Academic Reading 101

And Concurrent Development of Basic Presentation Skills

2

INTRODUCTION

INTRODUCTION TO ACADEMIC READING 101

ACADEMIC READING 101 is an exhaustive two-level series designed to help young adult learners of English thoroughly develop solid reading skills for future academic success. This series is both fundamental and comprehensive as it covers a wide range of academic content areas found in most typical first-year liberal arts courses. This series thereby promotes the enhancement of learners' ability to comprehend college-level texts by providing them with the opportunity to acquire and utilize a wide variety of effective reading and learning strategies.

In every respect, this series is ideal for learners who wish to develop advanced reading skills and expand their capability to demonstrate an in-depth understanding of challenging readings while also dramatically expanding their academic vocabulary. All in all, this series is not only a springboard in fulfilling personal language learning needs but, through its provision of varied and engaging subject matter, it allows learners to gain an accurate sense of the difficulty level of university courses through the study of topics that will undoubtedly prove interesting to the majority of students.

Furthermore, this series is replete with a rich array of post-reading activities that allow students to build on diverse reading skills: basic skills, reading skills, thinking skills, language skills, structure skills, communication skills and, finally, presentation skills. A notable benefit of this interplay of integrated reading skills is that it is proven to effectively advance learners' competency in building personal repertoires of effective reading strategies.

EXCEPTIONAL FEATURES

Academic topic selections used as a catalyst for first-year liberal arts courses

Communicative language teaching incorporated with presentation skills

Authentic and meaningful input to heighten learning and communication

Distinctive lesson development with two-tier reading passages in one themed unit

Encompassing prominent reading strategies and test-taking techniques

Motivating activities to capture learners' attention

Interactive reading tasks combining the bottom-up and top-down models

Conceptual and linguistic input embodied in post-reading activities

UNIT 1

LESSON 1.
Insight into Human Attraction

PRE-DISCUSSION FOCUS

1. Do you believe in love at first sight?

2. List five factors that you think make someone attractive.

MY LIST	MY PARTNER'S LIST

SCHEMA FOCUS

Read the statements below and write **T** for true, **F** for false or **NS** for what you are not sure of.
1. People around the world find boyfriends and girlfriends in similar ways.
2. People with similar ideas and beliefs tend to stay together longer.
3. Physical beauty is not important in attraction.
4. People are attracted to people who like them and to people they cannot have.
5. Women change their preferences in men as they grow older; young women like rich guys, but older women like men with strong-looking faces.

PRE-DISCUSSION FOCUS aims to generate learners' interest in the topic, through visual prompts and simple questions by sharing their ideas and experiences.

SCHEMA FOCUS activates learners' prior knowledge and relates personal experiences to the lesson theme. Five brief and informative statements enable them to build bridges between their existing knowledge and the new knowledge they will encounter throughout the lesson.

What Makes Someone Attractive?

Humans around the world find their boyfriends and girlfriends in very similar **ways**. In fact, baboons also find partners in a similar way. Who we love and how we love seem to be a part of **nature**. Culture also affects our choices. However, in general, people make similar decisions about whom to date.

Psychologists recognize five main **factors** that attract people to each other. First, proximity is important to attraction. Proximity means physical closeness. People **are more likely to be attracted to** people who are close to them. This is why people often like the girl or guy who **sits next to** them in class, but they do not even **notice** the girls or guys on the other side of the classroom.

It is also important that a potential boyfriend or girlfriend has many similar ideas or characteristics. People usually like others who **have something in common** with them. They like to share their similar ideas. If an idea is important to one partner, the other partner will probably share the opinion. If not, they may not stay together for very long. Also, people can spend more time together having fun if they enjoy doing the same things.

The third important factor is how familiar someone is. Usually people do not want to spend every moment with someone, but they do want to see a partner very often. Maybe that is why people usually like people who they see more often. In one study, a few beautiful girls attended a class almost every class period, and another group of beautiful girls attended the class just a few times. The boys said that girls who attended almost every class were more attractive.

People are also attracted to people who like them. If a girl likes a boy, he is more likely to be attracted to her than if she doesn't like him. This is probably because people feel good when others like them. People are more attracted to people who make them feel good.

Finally, people tend to like people they cannot have. Perhaps people just want a **challenge**. They may feel that the reward is better if they have to work to attract a potential boyfriend or girlfriend. Whatever the reason, many people are eager to date someone they cannot date.

FOCUSED READING

The Focused Reading section provides learners with resourceful information and adapted authentic language. The topic-specific language and fascinating knowledge covered in the text form the core of the first-year liberal arts course content. Each reading caters to learners' cognitive and linguistic levels.

LIBERAL ARTS — Psychology

Of course, physical beauty is another important factor of attraction. It is true that people in different cultures are attracted to different kinds of beauty. However, in general, people around the world agree on what is beautiful.

People are generally attracted to average faces. They also like faces that appear **balanced**. In one study, researchers took photographs of several different college girls. They used a computer to **average** their faces. Then, they showed the photos to several boys. The boys liked the average face that the computer made better than they liked the faces of the real girls.

However, there are certain looks that are more attractive than others. In girls, guys usually prefer faces that look young. Guys like girls with a baby face, but they also value faces that make a woman look more mature. For example, women with a wide smile are more attractive to many men.

In most cultures, men seek youth and beauty. Men like women who look healthy and have wide hips. They also prefer women who are young and have a lot of energy. Men might think that these women will be more fun. These women also seem more able to produce and raise healthy children.

Women change their preferences as they grow older. Young women who can have children often like men with strong-looking faces. They want to find a man who can **take care of** them and their children. However, as women become older, they change. Older women who can no longer have children prefer men with soft, kind faces.

Most women prefer men who are rich or powerful. Throughout history, men have always been women's superiors. Women have had less money than men, and it has been harder for women to find sufficient food. Women have always wanted to find men who can **provide** for them. They want men who can always give them and their children a safe place to live and enough food. Women today have more money than women in the past, but they still have less money than men on average. This might explain why most women focus on wealth and status.

RECALL FACTS
1. Do people tend to like people they see more or less often? Write the number "1" in the passage.
2. Why do people tend to like people who like them? Write the number "2" in the passage.
3. Is the perception of what is beautiful generally the same or different around the world? Write the number "3" in the passage.
4. What types of women do men generally prefer? Write the number "4" in the passage.
5. What types of men do women generally prefer? Write the number "5" in the passage.

IDENTIFY FACTS
1. Which of the following is **NOT** a factor in attraction discussed in the passage?
   a. physical closeness
   b. similar interests
   c. height
   d. frequent meetings
2. Which of the following types of girls would most men **NOT** like?
   a. a girl who looks young
   b. a girl who is very skinny
   c. a girl who looks healthy and has wide hips
   d. an energetic girl
3. What is the ideal amount of time for two people who are attracted to one another to see each other?
   a. rarely
   b. as often as possible
   c. often, but not too much
   d. all the time
4. Which of the following types of guys would most young women **NOT** like?
   a. a man good at taking care of people
   b. a man with a strong-looking face
   c. a rich and powerful man
   d. a young looking and energetic man
5. Which of the following statements is **NOT** true?
   a. People and monkeys find boyfriends and girlfriends in similar ways.
   b. People are attracted to people who like them.
   c. Culture does not affect who we date.
   d. People are attracted to beauty, and they generally agree on what is beautiful.

---

1 Basic Skills Focus

The **Basic Skills Focus** section consists of two parts, **RECALL FACTS** and **IDENTIFY FACTS**. This section asks learners to demonstrate basic comprehension by locating specific information in the text and to distinguish between indisputable facts and false information by employing eliminating skills.

2 Reading Skills Focus

The Reading Skills Focus section covers fundamental and diverse reading skills and strategies such as identifying **MAIN IDEA**, **AUTHOR'S PURPOSE**, **DETAIL**, **INFERENCE** and **CONTEXT CLUE**. This section enables learners to think deeply about the meaning of the text by focusing on the main ideas and important details of the text. Also, this section requires learners to go beyond reading comprehension to analyze each text and the author's intention.

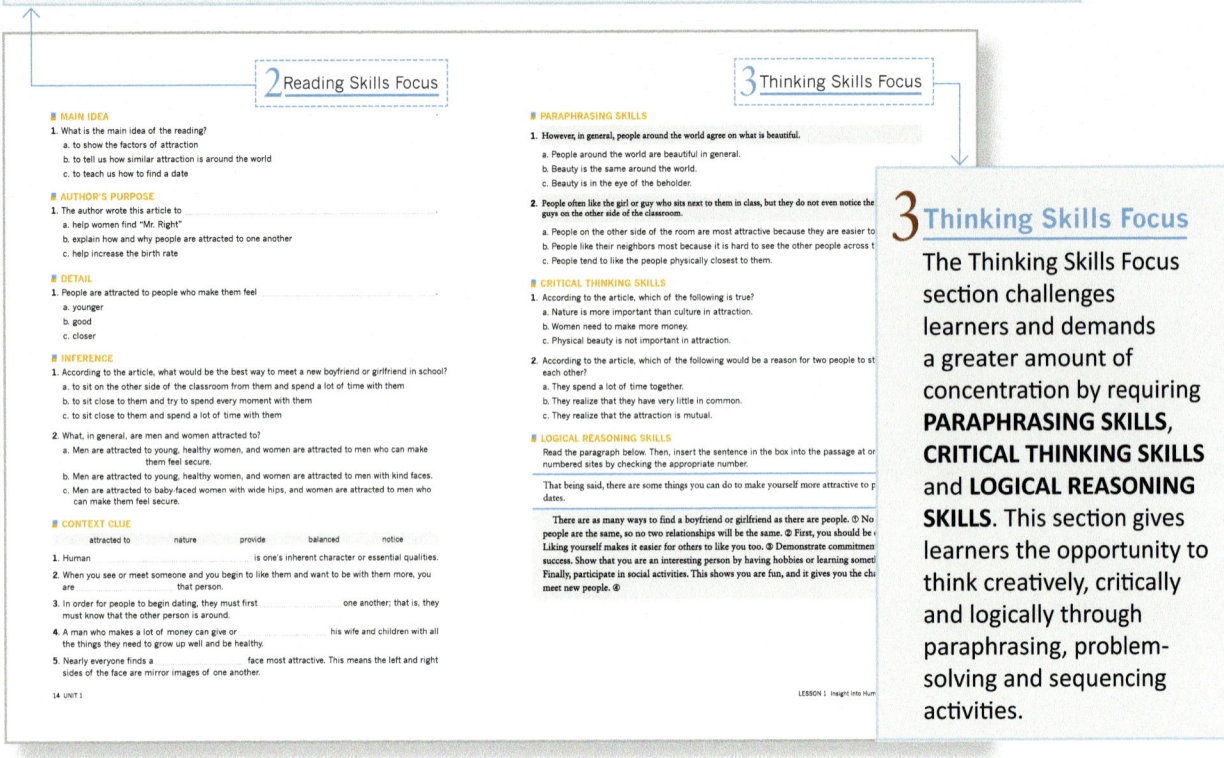

3 Thinking Skills Focus

The Thinking Skills Focus section challenges learners and demands a greater amount of concentration by requiring **PARAPHRASING SKILLS**, **CRITICAL THINKING SKILLS** and **LOGICAL REASONING SKILLS**. This section gives learners the opportunity to think creatively, critically and logically through paraphrasing, problem-solving and sequencing activities.

4 Language Skills Focus

The Language Skills Focus section is divided into **VOCABULARY DEFINITION**, which presents and reinforces high-frequency vocabulary items while building the understanding of semantics, and **LANGUAGE FORMS**, which clarifies linguistic forms.

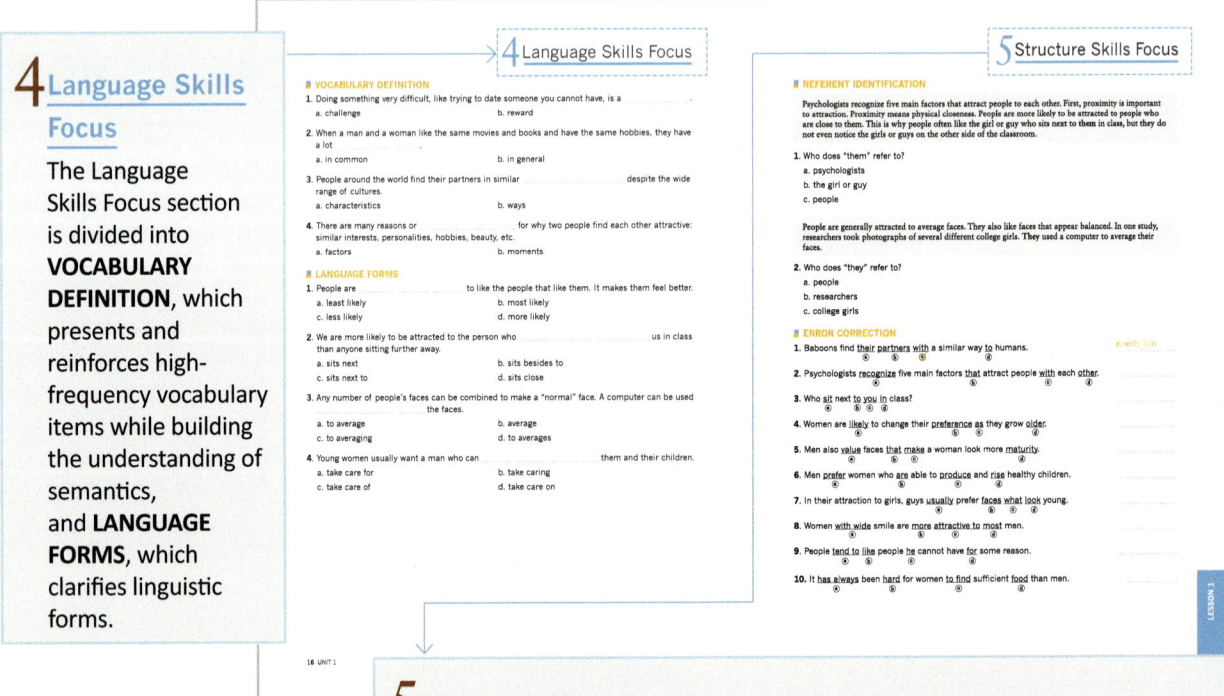

5 Structure Skills Focus

The Structure Skills Focus section is divided into **REFERENT IDENTIFICATION**, which develops the ability to evaluate the surrounding context to connect ideas, and **ERROR CORRECTION**, which clarifies linguistic structures so as to build the understanding of syntax. These two question types are commonly found on standardized tests such as TOEFL® and TOEIC®.

6 Communication Skills Focus

ACCURACY SKILLS
Answer the following questions by writing full sentences. Use the clues to help you come up with the correct answer.
1. What is one possible reason people are attracted to people they cannot have?
   • see • challenge

2. What may happen to a couple that does not share ideas and opinions?
   • not • stay together

FLUENCY SKILLS
Discuss your answers with a partner. Use the clues to help you come up with the correct answer.
1. What are the five factors psychologists recognize that attract people to each other?
   • proximity • familiar

2. How does culture affect what we think is beautiful?
   • different • similar

PERSONALIZING SKILLS
Answer the following questions with your own ideas in full sentences.
1. What do you think is the most important factor in what attracts people to one another?

2. Which do you think is more important in determining what is beautiful? Nature or culture?

Reinforcement Reading

Read the short passage below that expands on the reading at the beginning of the lesson. Then, cross out the unnecessary sentence by checking the box next to it.

Do Opposites Really Attract?

There is an old saying in English that "opposites attract." This seems to contradict the second factor psychologists mentioned in the passage. Opposites are not people who have similar ideas and characteristics. ☐ They are very different from us. ☐ Of course, you also have to actually meet the person and be in the same place at the same time. While you probably know some couples that are very different, recent research shows that we actually pick our boyfriends and girlfriends because they are very much like us but claim to want someone who is different. ☐ This is partly due to our genes. People tend to like others who have the same genetic characteristics. ☐ Genes may account for a third of the reason why we pick someone as a friend.

18 UNIT 1

---

6 Communication Skills Focus

The Communication Skills Focus section invigorates the lesson's fluency-and-accuracy-focused tasks through the parts titled, **ACCURACY SKILLS**, **FLUENCY SKILLS** and **PERSONALIZING SKILLS**. This section encourages learners to balance fluency and accuracy so that they can build communicative competence for successful communication in all academic settings.

7 Presentation Skills Focus

The Presentation Skills Focus section features four steps, **PLAN**, **PREPARE**, **PRACTICE** and **PERFORM** and helps equip learners with basic presentation skills and informative speech skills indispensable for most academic settings by revisiting the content covered in each lesson.

REINFORCEMENT READING

The Reinforcement Reading section again gives learners the opportunity to become fully engaged academic readers. This section allows students to expand further on the topic introduced in the primary reading as students are required to dissect a shorter passage related to the unit theme.

---

7 Presentation Skills Focus

Give a presentation using a visual aid.

STEP 1 PLAN
Put the situations in the box under the correct reason for attraction in the chart below.

Physical Closeness	Similar Ideas	Being Familiar	The Other Person Likes You	You Cannot Have the Other Person

SITUATIONS
ⓐ Both Jim and Serena attend church and go to an advanced English class.
ⓑ Sarah's best friend just told her that Tim has a crush on her.
ⓒ Mary is attracted to the new boy in class who was assigned to sit beside her in all her classes for the past month.
ⓓ Brian's mother told him that he can never date Tina.
ⓔ Mina and Frank were born in the same hospital, have been neighbors since they were five and have attended the same school for their entire lives.

Put the following traits under the correct heading. You may need to use some items more than once.

What Makes Women Attractive to Men	What Makes Men Attractive to Women

TRAITS
ⓐ youth ⓓ good provider ⓖ energetic attitude ⓙ balanced face ⓜ status
ⓑ strong-looking face ⓔ average face ⓗ wide hips ⓚ wealth
ⓒ health ⓕ baby face ⓘ soft, kind faces ⓛ beauty

STEP 2 PREPARE
Use the "Outline" chart below to prepare your presentation about "What Makes Men and Women Attracted to Each Other." You may prepare an outline by making some notes in the space below.

OUTLINE		
1. Introduction	**2. Body**	**3. Conclusion**

• Attention Getter/Hook
• Statement of Topic
• Overview
  - Main Point 1
  - Main Point 2
  - Main Point 3
	• Main Point 1
	  - Examples/Evidence
	• Main Point 2
	  - Examples/Evidence
	• Main Point 3
	  - Examples/Evidence
		• Restatement of Topic
		• Main Point 1
		  - Brief Review
		• Main Point 2
		  - Brief Review
		• Main Point 3
		  - Brief Review
		• Closing Comment

STEP 3 PRACTICE
Pair up. Then, deliver your presentation to each other.

STEP 4 PERFORM
Present your completed presentation to the class. Then, complete the peer evaluation record using a scale from 1 (lowest) to 5 (highest).

PEER EVALUATION RECORD
Presenter's Name:

Delivery	Grade				
Posture	1	2	3	4	5
Eye Contact	1	2	3	4	5
Gestures	1	2	3	4	5
Voice Inflection	1	2	3	4	5
Content	**Grade**				
Introduction	1	2	3	4	5
Body	1	2	3	4	5
Use of Evidence	1	2	3	4	5
Conclusion	1	2	3	4	5

CONTENTS

UNIT 1 — LIBERAL ARTS Psychology
THE PSYCHOLOGY OF ATTRACTION

Lesson 1 | Insight into Human Attraction ········· 10
- What Makes Someone Attractive? — *Focused Reading*
- Do Opposites Really Attract? — *Reinforcement Reading*

Lesson 2 | The Science of Attraction and Relationships ········· 20
- Moving from Attraction to Relationships — *Focused Reading*
- Physical Signs of Attraction — *Reinforcement Reading*

UNIT 1 REVIEW ········· 30

UNIT 2 — HUMANITIES Linguistics
ENGLISH AS A GLOBAL LANGUAGE

Lesson 3 | The Changing World of English ········· 32
- The Rise of English in the World — *Focused Reading*
- Language and Power — *Reinforcement Reading*

Lesson 4 | World Englishes and English Worlds ········· 42
- The Emergence of New Varieties of English — *Focused Reading*
- Different Purposes of Learning English — *Reinforcement Reading*

UNIT 2 REVIEW ········· 52

UNIT 3 — SOCIAL SCIENCES Sociology
HUMAN RIGHTS

Lesson 5 | The Basics of Human Rights ········· 54
- Fundamental Human Rights and the United Nations — *Focused Reading*
- The Magna Carta: The Cornerstone of Human Rights — *Reinforcement Reading*

Lesson 6 | The History of Human Rights ········· 64
- The Origins of Ideas about Human Rights — *Focused Reading*
- Mahatma Gandhi: Champion of Human Rights — *Reinforcement Reading*

UNIT 3 REVIEW ········· 74

UNIT 4　NATURAL SCIENCES　Earth Science
SOLAR SYSTEM

Lesson 7
The Inner Solar System ········ 76
Our Solar System: Inner Planets　*Focused Reading*
Amazing Facts about NASA's Mars Rover Curiosity　*Reinforcement Reading*

Lesson 8
The Outer Solar System ········ 86
Our Solar System: Outer Planets　*Focused Reading*
Interesting Facts about Comets　*Reinforcement Reading*

UNIT 4 REVIEW ········ 96

UNIT 5　BUSINESS & ECONOMICS　Economics
TRADE IN THE PAST AND MODERN TIMES

Lesson 9
The Silk Road ········ 98
The Legacy of the Silk Road　*Focused Reading*
Marco Polo: Silk Road Traveler and Explorer　*Reinforcement Reading*

Lesson 10
Protectionism vs. Free Trade ········ 108
Global Exchange: Protectionism and Free Trade　*Focused Reading*
Challenges for China in the World Trade　*Reinforcement Reading*

UNIT 5 REVIEW ········ 118

UNIT 6　FINE ARTS & MUSIC　A History of Art and Music
FROM RENAISSANCE TO BAROQUE

Lesson 11
The Renaissance Era ········ 120
Renaissance Art and Music　*Focused Reading*
Leonardo da Vinci: The Famed Renaissance Man　*Reinforcement Reading*

Lesson 12
The Baroque Era ········ 130
Baroque Art and Music　*Focused Reading*
Bach and Handel: The Two Giants of Baroque Music　*Reinforcement Reading*

UNIT 6 REVIEW ········ 140

UNIT 1

THE PSYCHOLOGY OF ATTRACTION

Lesson 1. Insight into Human Attraction
- Focused Reading — What Makes Someone Attractive?
- Reinforcement Reading — Do Opposites Really Attract?

Lesson 2. The Science of Attraction and Relationships
- Focused Reading — Moving from Attraction to Relationships
- Reinforcement Reading — Physical Signs of Attraction

UNIT 1

LESSON 1.
Insight into Human Attraction

■ **PRE-DISCUSSION FOCUS**

1. Do you believe in love at first sight?
   ....

2. List five factors that you think make someone attractive.

MY LIST	MY PARTNER'S LIST

■ **SCHEMA FOCUS**

Read the statements below and write **T** for true, **F** for false or **NS** for what you are not sure of.

1. People around the world find boyfriends and girlfriends in similar ways.
2. People with similar ideas and beliefs tend to stay together longer.
3. Physical beauty is not important in attraction.
4. People are attracted to people who like them and to people they cannot have.
5. Women change their preferences in men as they grow older; young women like righ guys, but older women like men with strong-looking faces.

What Makes Someone Attractive?

Humans around the world find their boyfriends and girlfriends in very similar **ways**. In fact, baboons also find partners in a similar way. Who we love and how we love seem to be a part of **nature**. Culture also affects our choices. However, in general, people make similar decisions about whom to date.

Psychologists recognize five main **factors** that attract people to each other. First, proximity is important to attraction. Proximity means physical closeness. People **are more likely to** be **attracted to** people who are close to them. This is why people often like the girl or guy who **sits next to** them in class, but they do not even **notice** the girls or guys on the other side of the classroom.

It is also important that a potential boyfriend or girlfriend has many similar ideas or characteristics. People usually like others who **have** something **in common** with them. They like to share their similar ideas. If an idea is important to one partner, the other partner will probably share the opinion. If not, they may not stay together for very long. Also, people can spend more time together having fun if they enjoy doing the same things.

The third important factor is how familiar someone is. Usually people do not want to spend every moment with someone, but they do want to see a partner very often. Maybe that is why people usually like people who they see more often. In one study, a few beautiful girls attended a class almost every class period, and another group of beautiful girls attended the class just a few times. The boys said that girls who attended almost every class were more attractive.

People are also attracted to people who like them. If a girl likes a boy, he is more likely to be attracted to her than if she doesn't like him. This is probably because people feel good when others like them. People are more attracted to people who make them feel good.

Finally, people tend to like people they cannot have. Perhaps people just want a **challenge**. They may feel that the reward is better if they have to work to attract a potential boyfriend or girlfriend. Whatever the reason, many people are eager to date someone they cannot date.

LIBERAL ARTS
Psychology

Of course, physical beauty is another important factor of attraction. It is true that people in different cultures are attracted to different kinds of beauty. However, in general, people around the world agree on what is beautiful.

People are generally attracted to average faces. They also like faces that appear **balanced**. In one study, researchers took photographs of several different college girls. They used a computer to **average** their faces. Then, they showed the photos to several boys. The boys liked the average face that the computer made better than they liked the faces of the real girls.

However, there are certain looks that are more attractive than others. In girls, guys usually prefer faces that look young. Guys like girls with a baby face, but they also value faces that make a woman look more mature. For example, women with a wide smile are more attractive to many men.

In most cultures, men seek youth and beauty. Men like women who look healthy and have wide hips. They also prefer women who are young and have a lot of energy. Men might think that these women will be more fun. These women also seem more able to produce and raise healthy children.

Women change their preferences as they grow older. Young women who can have children often like men with strong-looking faces. They want to find a man who can **take care of** them and their children. However, as women become older, they change. Older women who can no longer have children prefer men with soft, kind faces.

Most women prefer men who are rich or powerful. Throughout history, men have always been women's superiors. Women have had less money than men, and it has been harder for women to find sufficient food. Women have always wanted to find men who can **provide** for them. They want men who can always give them and their children a safe place to live and enough food. Women today have more money than women in the past, but they still have less money than men on average. This might explain why most women focus on wealth and status.

1 Basic Skills Focus

■ RECALL FACTS

1. Do people tend to like people they see more or less often? Write the number "1" in the passage.

2. Why do people tend to like people who like them? Write the number "2" in the passage.

3. Is the perception of what is beautiful generally the same or different around the world? Write the number "3" in the passage.

4. What types of women do men generally prefer? Write the number "4" in the passage.

5. What types of men do women generally prefer? Write the number "5" in the passage.

■ IDENTIFY FACTS

1. Which of the following is **NOT** a factor in attraction discussed in the passage?
   a. physical closeness
   b. similar interests
   c. height
   d. frequent meetings

2. Which of the following types of girls would most men **NOT** like?
   a. a girl who looks young
   b. a girl who is very skinny
   c. a girl who looks healthy and has wide hips
   d. an energetic girl

3. What is the ideal amount of time for two people who are attracted to one another to see each other?
   a. rarely
   b. as often as possible
   c. often, but not too much
   d. all the time

4. Which of the following types of guys would most young women **NOT** like?
   a. a man good at taking care of people
   b. a man with a strong-looking face
   c. a rich and powerful man
   d. a young looking and energetic man

5. Which of the following statements is **NOT** true?
   a. People and monkeys find boyfriends and girlfriends in similar ways.
   b. People are attracted to people who like them.
   c. Culture does not affect who we date.
   d. People are attracted to beauty, and they generally agree on what is beautiful.

2 Reading Skills Focus

■ MAIN IDEA

1. What is the main idea of the reading?
    a. to show the factors of attraction
    b. to tell us how similar attraction is around the world
    c. to teach us how to find a date

■ AUTHOR'S PURPOSE

1. The author wrote this article to ....
    a. help women find "Mr. Right"
    b. explain how and why people are attracted to one another
    c. help increase the birth rate

■ DETAIL

1. People are attracted to people who make them feel ....
    a. younger
    b. good
    c. closer

■ INFERENCE

1. According to the article, what would be the best way to meet a new boyfriend or girlfriend in school?
    a. to sit on the other side of the classroom from them and spend a lot of time with them
    b. to sit close to them and try to spend every moment with them
    c. to sit close to them and spend a lot of time with them

2. What, in general, are men and women attracted to?
    a. Men are attracted to young, healthy women, and women are attracted to men who can make them feel secure.
    b. Men are attracted to young, healthy women, and women are attracted to men with kind faces.
    c. Men are attracted to baby-faced women with wide hips, and women are attracted to men who can make them feel secure.

■ CONTEXT CLUE

| attracted to | nature | provide | balanced | notice |

1. Human .... is one's inherent character or essential qualities.

2. When you see or meet someone and you begin to like them and want to be with them more, you are .... that person.

3. In order for people to begin dating, they must first .... one another; that is, they must know that the other person is around.

4. A man who makes a lot of money can give or .... his wife and children with all the things they need to grow up well and be healthy.

5. Nearly everyone finds a .... face most attractive. This means the left and right sides of the face are mirror images of one another.

14 UNIT 1

3 Thinking Skills Focus

■ PARAPHRASING SKILLS

1. However, in general, people around the world agree on what is beautiful.

   a. People around the world are beautiful in general.
   b. Beauty is the same around the world.
   c. Beauty is in the eye of the beholder.

2. People often like the girl or guy who sits next to them in class, but they do not even notice the girls or guys on the other side of the classroom.

   a. People on the other side of the room are most attractive because they are easier to see.
   b. People like their neighbors most because it is hard to see the other people across the room.
   c. People tend to like the people physically closest to them.

■ CRITICAL THINKING SKILLS

1. According to the article, which of the following is true?
   a. Nature is more important than culture in attraction.
   b. Women need to make more money.
   c. Physical beauty is not important in attraction.

2. According to the article, which of the following would be a reason for two people to stop seeing each other?
   a. They spend a lot of time together.
   b. They realize that they have very little in common.
   c. They realize that the attraction is mutual.

■ LOGICAL REASONING SKILLS

Read the paragraph below. Then, insert the sentence in the box into the passage at one of the numbered sites by checking the appropriate number.

That being said, there are some things you can do to make yourself more attractive to potential dates.

There are as many ways to find a boyfriend or girlfriend as there are people. ① No two people are the same, so no two relationships will be the same. ② First, you should be confident. Liking yourself makes it easier for others to like you too. ③ Demonstrate commitment and success. Show that you are an interesting person by having hobbies or learning something new. Finally, participate in social activities. This shows you are fun, and it gives you the chance to meet new people. ④

4 Language Skills Focus

■ VOCABULARY DEFINITION

1. Doing something very difficult, like trying to date someone you cannot have, is a ....
   a. challenge
   b. reward

2. When a man and a woman like the same movies and books and have the same hobbies, they have a lot ....
   a. in common
   b. in general

3. People around the world find their partners in similar .... despite the wide range of cultures.
   a. characteristics
   b. ways

4. There are many reasons or .... for why two people find each other attractive: similar interests, personalities, hobbies, beauty, etc.
   a. factors
   b. moments

■ LANGUAGE FORMS

1. People are .... to like the people that like them. It makes them feel better.
   a. least likely
   b. most likely
   c. less likely
   d. more likely

2. We are more likely to be attracted to the person who .... us in class than anyone sitting further away.
   a. sits next
   b. sits besides to
   c. sits next to
   d. sits close

3. Any number of people's faces can be combined to make a "normal" face. A computer can be used .... the faces.
   a. to average
   b. average
   c. to averaging
   d. to averages

4. Young women usually want a man who can .... them and their children.
   a. take care for
   b. take caring
   c. take care of
   d. take care on

16 UNIT 1

5 Structure Skills Focus

■ REFERENT IDENTIFICATION

Psychologists recognize five main factors that attract people to each other. First, proximity is important to attraction. Proximity means physical closeness. People are more likely to be attracted to people who are close to them. This is why people often like the girl or guy who sits next to **them** in class, but they do not even notice the girls or guys on the other side of the classroom.

1. Who does "them" refer to?
   a. psychologists
   b. the girl or guy
   c. people

People are generally attracted to average faces. They also like faces that appear balanced. In one study, researchers took photographs of several different college girls. **They** used a computer to average their faces.

2. Who does "they" refer to?
   a. people
   b. researchers
   c. college girls

■ ERROR CORRECTION

1. Baboons find <u>their</u> <u>partners</u> <u>with</u> a similar way <u>to</u> humans.   ⓒ with → in
                   ⓐ   ⓑ   ⓒ   ⓓ

2. Psychologists <u>recognize</u> five main factors <u>that</u> attract people <u>with</u> each <u>other</u>.
                          ⓐ   ⓑ   ⓒ   ⓓ

3. Who <u>sit</u> next <u>to</u> <u>you</u> <u>in</u> class?
           ⓐ   ⓑ ⓒ ⓓ

4. Women are <u>likely</u> to change their <u>preference</u> <u>as</u> they grow <u>older</u>.
                  ⓐ   ⓑ   ⓒ   ⓓ

5. Men also <u>value</u> faces <u>that</u> <u>make</u> a woman look more <u>maturity</u>.
             ⓐ   ⓑ   ⓒ   ⓓ

6. Men <u>prefer</u> women who <u>are</u> able to <u>produce</u> and <u>rise</u> healthy children.
          ⓐ   ⓑ   ⓒ   ⓓ

7. In their attraction to girls, guys <u>usually</u> prefer <u>faces</u> <u>what</u> <u>look</u> young.
                                     ⓐ   ⓑ   ⓒ   ⓓ

8. Women <u>with wide</u> smile are <u>more</u> <u>attractive to</u> <u>most</u> men.
               ⓐ   ⓑ   ⓒ   ⓓ

9. People <u>tend to</u> <u>like</u> people <u>he</u> cannot have <u>for</u> some reason.
             ⓐ   ⓑ   ⓒ   ⓓ

10. It <u>has always</u> been <u>hard</u> for women <u>to find</u> sufficient <u>food</u> than men.
           ⓐ   ⓑ   ⓒ   ⓓ

6 Communication Skills Focus

■ ACCURACY SKILLS

Answer the following questions by writing full sentences. Use the clues to help you come up with the correct answer.

1. What is one possible reason people are attracted to people they cannot have?
   • see • challenge

2. What may happen to a couple that does not share ideas and opinions?
   • not • stay together

■ FLUENCY SKILLS

Discuss your answers with a partner. Use the clues to help you come up with the correct answer.

1. What are the five factors psychologists recognize that attract people to each other?
   • proximity • familiar

2. How does culture affect what we think is beautiful?
   • different • similar

■ PERSONALIZING SKILLS

Answer the following questions with your own ideas in full sentences.

1. What do you think is the most important factor in what attracts people to one another?

2. Which do you think is more important in determining what is beautiful? Nature or culture?

Reinforcement Reading

Read the short passage below that expands on the reading at the beginning of the lesson. Then, cross out the unnecessary sentence by checking the box next to it.

Do Opposites Really Attract?

There is an old saying in English that "opposites attract." This seems to contradict the second factor psychologists mentioned in the passage. Opposites are not people who have similar ideas and characteristics. ☐ They are very different from us. ☐ Of course, you also have to actually meet the person and be in the same place at the same time. While you probably know some couples that are very different, recent research shows that we actually pick our boyfriends and girlfriends because they are very much like us but claim to want someone who is different. ☐ This is partly due to our genes. People tend to like others who have the same genetic characteristics. ☐ Genes may account for a third of the reason why we pick someone as a friend.

7 Presentation Skills Focus

■ Give a presentation using a visual aid.

STEP 1 PLAN
Put the situations in the box under the correct reason for attraction in the chart below.

Physical Closeness	Similar Ideas	Being Familiar	The Other Person Likes You	You Cannot Have the Other Person

SITUATIONS
ⓐ Both Jim and Serena attend church and go to an advanced English class.
ⓑ Sarah's best friend just told her that Tim has a crush on her.
ⓒ Mary is attracted to the new boy in class who was assigned to sit beside her in all her classes for the past month.
ⓓ Brian's mother told him that he can never date Tina.
ⓔ Mina and Frank were born in the same hospital, have been neighbors since they were five and have attended the same school for their entire lives.

Put the following traits under the correct heading. You may need to use some items more than once.

What Makes Women Attractive to Men	What Makes Men Attractive to Women

TRAITS
ⓐ youth　　ⓓ good provider　　ⓖ energetic attitude　　ⓙ balanced face　　ⓜ status
ⓑ strong-looking face　　ⓔ average face　　ⓗ wide hips　　ⓚ wealth
ⓒ health　　ⓕ baby face　　ⓘ soft, kind faces　　ⓛ beauty

STEP 2 PREPARE
Use the "Outline" chart below to prepare your presentation about "What Makes Men and Women Attracted to Each Other." You may prepare an outline by making some notes in the space below.

OUTLINE		
1. Introduction	**2. Body**	**3. Conclusion**
• Attention Getter/Hook • Statement of Topic • Overview 　- Main Point 1 　- Main Point 2 　- Main Point 3	• Main Point 1 　- Examples/Evidence • Main Point 2 　- Examples/Evidence • Main Point 3 　- Examples/Evidence	• Restatement of Topic • Main Point 1 　- Brief Review • Main Point 2 　- Brief Review • Main Point 3 　- Brief Review • Closing Comment

STEP 3 PRACTICE
Pair up. Then, deliver your presentation to each other.

STEP 4 PERFORM
Present your completed presentation to the class. Then, complete the peer evaluation record using a scale from 1 (lowest) to 5 (highest).

PEER EVALUATION RECORD
Presenter's Name: _____

Delivery	Grade				
Posture	1	2	3	4	5
Eye Contact	1	2	3	4	5
Gestures	1	2	3	4	5
Voice Inflection	1	2	3	4	5
Content	**Grade**				
Introduction	1	2	3	4	5
Body	1	2	3	4	5
Use of Evidence	1	2	3	4	5
Conclusion	1	2	3	4	5

UNIT 1

LESSON 2.
The Science of Attraction and Relationships

■ **PRE-DISCUSSION FOCUS**

1. What kind of person do you find attractive?

2. What do you think some of the steps are in moving from attraction to dating?

MY LIST	MY PARTNER'S LIST

■ **SCHEMA FOCUS**

Read the statements below and write **T** for true, **F** for false or **NS** for what you are not sure of.

1. Some researchers believe people have "love maps" which help them find their boyfriends or girlfriends.
2. You need a lot of attraction points if you want to find a boyfriend or girlfriend.
3. Two people beginning a relationship will start to move in different ways.
4. People tend to date others that are about as physically attractive as they are.
5. Women will giggle and look away from people they are not attracted to.

FOCUSED READING
🎧 02

Moving from Attraction to Relationships

With so many factors at play, it may seem difficult to decide who is the best person to date. In other ways it seems like this decision must just be chance. In fact, people have **specific** ways of choosing their partners.

One researcher, John Money, says that people have a "love map." This love map helps people decide what attracts them to another person. A love map is an individual's personal perception of what their ideal partner should look like and how they should act and behave. A love map description consists of specific details such as one's race, facial features, personality, and physical build among other characteristics. A love map is stored in the brain, and everyone's love map is a little different. This idea of a love map can also explain why everyone seems to be attracted to different people. It is common to meet a couple and think, "What do they see in each other?" This is a sure **sign** that every individual is using a very different love map to **evaluate** one another.

Attraction points are another way to understand how all of these factors work together. According to this theory, people assign points for every factor that they think is attractive. People with more points are more attractive. In this case, the total number of points is more important than the score in any one area.

Most people are aware of how many attraction points they have. People usually know how beautiful or handsome they are and how much they attract others. Normally, people choose to date other people with a similar number of attraction points.

Even after people know what kind of person they are attracted to, they still have to find an attractive person. Then, they have to find a way to start a **relationship** with that person. There are many different ways to do this, but they all follow certain **patterns**.

At any social event in any country, people tend to follow a certain pattern to attract a partner. First, they find an area in the room where they are comfortable. Girls tend to find a place in a group of girls because this makes them look more attractive. Guys also look more attractive when they **are surrounded by** girls.

Then, the girls and the guys both try to attract attention. They try to make other people look at them. Guys move their arms more than they need to. They do everything **in an exaggerated way**. Girls do many of the same things, but they may also play with their hair or do something else to **draw attention to** their beauty.

After someone **catches the attention of** a possible partner, that person will **look into** the other **person's eyes**. This look is a kind of a direct question. When someone looks at a possible partner this way, the possible partner will make a choice. He or she will either come closer or **turn away**. This makes it clear that a relationship is possible or that a relationship can never work.

If the potential partner chooses to talk to the person, they will start to try to impress each other. Men will move their chests forward to show power. Women will smile and look at the man before looking away and giggling.

As the two decide to get to know each other, another change happens. Their shoulders turn towards each other. After a while, their shoulders **line up**. Then, they start to move in the same way. If one of them moves their right arm, the other will too. From this point, they may decide to become boyfriend and girlfriend.

However, they still have to be careful. If they move too fast, one partner may become frightened and stop the relationship. So, it is generally better to take a relationship very slowly.

This initial strong attraction will usually last between eighteen months and three years. After that time, the attraction is not as strong. Partners may begin to become interested in other people. Especially if they are young and do not have any children, married couples may divorce at this point. This might explain why many marriages around the world end after four years.

Attraction has many factors and is a long process. It is not surprising that people find attraction so **mysterious**. Although researchers have found many explanations, attraction will probably always be surrounded in mystery.

1 Basic Skills Focus

■ RECALL FACTS

1. Where is a "love map" stored? Write the number "1" in the passage.

2. What is an attraction point? Write the number "2" in the passage.

3. What is the first step in starting a relationship with someone you find attractive? Write the number "3" in the passage.

4. How do guys attract attention to themselves? Write the number "4" in the passage.

5. How long does the initial strong attraction between two people usually last? Write the number "5" in the passage.

■ IDENTIFY FACTS

1. Which of the following is **NOT** true of the "love map" theory?
    a. It is stored in the brain.
    b. It helps people decide who they like.
    c. It explains why we are all attracted to different people.
    d. It shows us how to meet someone.

2. Which of the following is **NOT** true of the "attraction points" theory?
    a. People assign points for every factor they like in another person.
    b. The total number of points is more important than the number in any one area.
    c. People with fewer points are more attractive.
    d. People usually end up with someone with about the same number of attraction points.

3. Which of the following is **NOT** a way to try and attract attention?
    a. moving in an exaggerated way
    b. looking directly into someone's eyes
    c. playing with your hair
    d. moving your arms more than necessary

4. How does a woman try to impress a man she is attracted to?
    a. She talks quickly.
    b. She smiles at him.
    c. She never looks into his eyes.
    d. She moves her chests forward to show power.

5. Why do many people get divorced after four years?
    a. Because they cannot have children.
    b. Because they moved too fast.
    c. Because their shoulders no longer line up.
    d. Because they lose their initial attraction.

2 Reading Skills Focus

■ MAIN IDEA

1. What is the main idea of the reading?
   a. to explain that attraction and dating are complicated and mysterious but follow certain patterns around the world
   b. to explain how the "love map" and "attraction points" theories work
   c. to teach people how to act at a social gathering so that they can attract attention and find a date

■ AUTHOR'S PURPOSE

1. The author wrote this article to ....
   a. warn people not to move too quickly when they are dating
   b. show people how to be more attractive to the opposite gender
   c. explain how people move from attraction to dating

■ DETAIL

1. What was **NOT** mentioned in the passage as a detail that may be found on a love map?
   a. physical build
   b. race
   c. talent

■ INFERENCE

1. Why is it better to take relationships slowly?
   a. Because if you don't, one of the people in the relationship may become scared and want to stop.
   b. Because if you don't, the three years of attraction will be over even sooner.
   c. Because a "love map" cannot move quickly.

2. Which of the following is true according to the article?
   a. Giggling makes women look cute and therefore attractive to men.
   b. Attraction has always been mysterious and probably always will be.
   c. It is not possible to know or change how many love points you have.

■ CONTEXT CLUE

patterns	catches	specific	mysterious	relationship

1. Because people around the world tend to act in similar ways, researchers have been able to find .... of dating behavior.

2. The passage describes the steps two people might go through in starting a ....

3. Although we may not realize it, we have detailed and .... ways of choosing our partners.

4. Attraction, dating and love are all .... No one understands how they work.

5. He always .... the attention of the girls by talking very loudly and moving his arms a lot. He behaves in an exaggerated way.

3 Thinking Skills Focus

■ PARAPHRASING SKILLS

1. People usually know how beautiful or handsome they are and how much they attract others.

   a. How beautiful you are determines how much you attract others.
   b. People are usually aware of how attractive they are.
   c. Beautiful and handsome people are attracted to one another.

2. Even after people know what kind of person they are attracted to, they still have to find an attractive person. Then, they have to find a way to start a relationship with that person.

   a. First you are attracted to someone, and then you find a way to meet them.
   b. Even attractive people have to find ways to begin relationships.
   c. People know who they are attracted to, but the problem is they cannot talk to those people.

■ CRITICAL THINKING SKILLS

1. According to the "love map" theory, how do people usually end up dating people with about the same number of points as themselves?

   a. Because opposites attract.
   b. Most people are well aware of their attractiveness.
   c. Because unattractive people do not want to date attractive people.

2. If a man finds a woman attractive and the woman finds the man attractive, why would **NOT** the two of them start dating?

   a. They need to catch one another's attention first.
   b. They may be afraid of taking things too fast.
   c. They still have to have the courage to talk to one another.

■ LOGICAL REASONING SKILLS

Read the paragraph below. Then, insert the sentence in the box into the passage at one of the numbered sites by checking the appropriate number.

> Beauty is also important, especially for women.

Although we might expect that what a person finds attractive is based on his or her culture, this is not the case. ① What is attractive seems to be a part of our nature. Psychologists have found five factors that make someone attractive: how close someone is to you, how similar their ideas and character, how familiar they are, if they like you and whether or not you can have them. ② The ability to provide is important in men. ③ These factors would count as attraction points in the "love map" theory of attraction. If someone has enough of them and you find them attractive, you would try and get their attention. After that, if you begin talking and getting to know one another, you may move on to dating. ④ Initial attractions usually only last between eighteen months and three years, so if you want your relationship to last longer, you will have to be careful and work hard at it.

4 Language Skills Focus

■ VOCABULARY DEFINITION

1. If someone moves more and faster than they need to or if they speak louder than is necessary, we say they are acting in an _____ way.

   a. exaggerated   b. initial

2. While a test is often used to _____ students, attraction points may be used to decide who the most attractive person to date is.

   a. impress   b. evaluate

3. If two people look into one another's eyes for a long time, sit directly facing one another, make similar movements and smile and laugh a lot, it is a sure _____ they find one another attractive.

   a. sign   b. perception

4. She was looking at my friend and we thought she was interested, but then she _____ and began to talk to her friends.

   a. divorced   b. turned away

■ LANGUAGE FORMS

1. According to the passage, both men and women are seen as more attractive when they are _____ women.

   a. surrounding by   b. surround by
   c. surrounded for   d. surrounded by

2. A woman who is interested in a man may play with her hair to _____ her beauty.

   a. drawing attention to   b. drawing attentions for
   c. draw attention to   d. draw attentions for

3. _____ someone's eyes can be a kind of direct question like "Do you find me attractive?"

   a. Looking at   b. Looking for
   c. Looking into   d. Looking away

4. What does it mean when two people's shoulders begin to _____?

   a. be lined up   b. line up
   c. be in a line   d. lining up

26 UNIT 1

5 Structure Skills Focus

■ REFERENT IDENTIFICATION

After someone catches the attention of a possible partner, that person will look into the other person's eyes. This look is a kind of a direct question. When someone looks at a possible partner this way, the possible partner will make a choice. He or she will either come closer or turn away. **This** makes it clear that a relationship is possible or that a relationship can never work.

1. What does "this" refer to?
   a. catching the attention of a possible partner
   b. looking at a possible partner
   c. either coming closer or turning away

As the man and woman decide to get to know each other, another change happens. Their shoulders turn towards each other. After a while, their shoulders line up. Then, they start to move in the same way. If one of **them** moves their right arm, the other will too.

2. Who does "them" refer to?
   a. the man and woman
   b. each other
   c. shoulders

■ ERROR CORRECTION

1. It is <u>often</u> difficult <u>decide</u> <u>who</u> <u>to</u> date.
          ⓐ   ⓑ   ⓒ ⓓ

2. One theory <u>of dating</u> says <u>that</u> all people have <u>love</u> map in <u>their</u> brains.
               ⓐ   ⓑ   ⓒ   ⓓ

3. Sometimes <u>it</u> <u>is</u> hard <u>to see</u> why a <u>couples</u> is together.
              ⓐⓑ   ⓒ   ⓓ

4. <u>What</u> kind of person <u>are</u> you <u>most</u> <u>attracted</u>?
    ⓐ   ⓑ   ⓒ   ⓓ

5. Most people are <u>aware</u> of how <u>much</u> <u>attraction</u> points they <u>have</u>.
                    ⓐ   ⓑ   ⓒ   ⓓ

6. People usually know <u>how</u> beautiful <u>and</u> handsome <u>they are</u> and how much <u>they</u> attract others.
                        ⓐ   ⓑ   ⓒ
        ⓓ

7. Everyone <u>looks</u> <u>more</u> attractive <u>when</u> they are surrounded <u>with</u> girls.
             ⓐ   ⓑ   ⓒ   ⓓ

8. <u>Some</u> people <u>say</u> they don't know <u>what</u> she sees <u>at</u> him.
   ⓐ   ⓑ   ⓒ   ⓓ

9. They talked <u>to</u> one another <u>for</u> 20 minutes <u>before</u> their shoulders <u>line</u> up.
             ⓐ   ⓑ   ⓒ   ⓓ

10. It is not <u>surprised</u> that people <u>find</u> attraction <u>so</u> <u>mysterious</u>.
               ⓐ   ⓑ   ⓒ   ⓓ

LESSON 2 The Science of Attraction and Relationships

6 Communication Skills Focus

■ ACCURACY SKILLS

Answer the following questions by writing full sentences. Use the clues to help you come up with the correct answer.

1. What are attraction points?
   • points • attractive

2. According to the passage, what is the first step in finding a date at a social event?
   • find • comfortable area

■ FLUENCY SKILLS

Discuss your answers with a partner. Use the clues to help you come up with the correct answer.

1. As two people get to know each other, what happens while they are talking?
   • shoulders • line up

2. What is one way the passage mentions a relationship may be ended?
   • move • too fast

■ PERSONALIZING SKILLS

Answer the following questions with your own ideas in full sentences.

1. Based on the idea of the "love map" that was introduced in the reading, in as much specific detail as possible, how would you describe your ideal partner?

2. Of the steps in moving from attraction to dating: getting comfortable, attracting attention, deciding to get to know the other person, trying to impress the other person and getting to know the other person, which is the most difficult and why?

Reinforcement Reading

Read the short passage below that expands on the reading at the beginning of the lesson. Then, cross out the unnecessary sentence by checking the box next to it.

Physical Signs of Attraction

Men and women use many of the same signs to show whether or not they are interested in someone. ☐ Most of our body language is subconscious. Any time someone points their feet, legs or arms toward you when they are talking to you, it may be an indication of interest. ☐ Crossed arms or looking away means the person is not interested. ☐ If someone maintains eye contact with you, it is also a good sign of interest. "Accidental" touches on the arm or shoulder are another way both men and women show their interest. ☐ Men will also stand up straight and may put their hands on their hips. Women will smile and play with their hair.

7 Presentation Skills Focus

■ Give a presentation using a visual aid.

STEP 1 PLAN
Put the steps of moving from attraction to dating in order.

PROCESS

1.
2.
3.
4.
5.
6.
7.
8.
9.
10.

FACTORS

ⓐ Talk to the person.
ⓑ Impress the other person.
ⓒ Look into the eyes of the person you like.
ⓓ Attend a social event.
ⓔ Take a relationship very slowly and become boyfriend and girlfriend.
ⓕ Get to know the person better.
ⓖ Find someone you like with about the same number of attraction points as yourself.
ⓗ Line up your shoulders and body with the other person.
ⓘ Attract attention by making exaggerated movements.
ⓙ Get closer to the person whose eyes you looked into.

STEP 2 PREPARE
Use the "Outline" chart below to prepare your presentation about "Moving from Attraction to Relationships." You may prepare an outline by making some notes in the space below.

OUTLINE		
1. Introduction	**2. Body**	**3. Conclusion**

• Attention Getter/Hook
• Statement of Topic
• Overview
  · Main Point 1
  · Main Point 2
  · Main Point 3
	• Main Point 1
	  · Examples/Evidence
	• Main Point 2
	  · Examples/Evidence
	• Main Point 3
	  · Examples/Evidence
		• Restatement of Topic
		• Main Point 1
		  · Brief Review
		• Main Point 2
		  · Brief Review
		• Main Point 3
		  · Brief Review
		• Closing Comment

STEP 3 PRACTICE
Pair up. Then, deliver your presentation to each other.

STEP 4 PERFORM
Present your completed presentation to the class. Then, complete the peer evaluation record using a scale from 1 (lowest) to 5 (highest).

PEER EVALUATION RECORD
Presenter's Name: _____

Delivery	Grade				
Posture	1	2	3	4	5
Eye Contact	1	2	3	4	5
Gestures	1	2	3	4	5
Voice Inflection	1	2	3	4	5
Content	**Grade**				
Introduction	1	2	3	4	5
Body	1	2	3	4	5
Use of Evidence	1	2	3	4	5
Conclusion	1	2	3	4	5

UNIT 1 REVIEW

INFORMATION ORGANIZATION

Take a close look at the factors of attraction and put the factors by gender into the correct part of the first chart. Then, sort out the relationship process into the correct part of the second chart.

GENDER COMPARISONS IN ATTRACTION AND RELATIONSHIPS

THE FACTORS OF ATTRACTION

- ⓐ rich
- ⓑ powerful
- ⓒ healthy
- ⓓ likes you
- ⓔ soft, kind face
- ⓕ beautiful
- ⓖ good provider
- ⓗ can't have the person
- ⓘ young
- ⓙ nice smile
- ⓚ familiar
- ⓛ wide hips
- ⓜ energetic
- ⓝ close to you
- ⓞ strong-looking face
- ⓟ share similar ideas and character

MEN	MEN AND WOMEN	WOMEN

THE RELATIONSHIP PROCESS

- ⓐ enough attraction points
- ⓑ get comfortable (surrounded by girls)
- ⓒ attract attention
- ⓓ move your arms
- ⓔ exaggerate your movements
- ⓕ giggle
- ⓖ play with your hair
- ⓗ look into the person's eyes
- ⓘ move closer
- ⓙ talk to the person
- ⓚ move your chest forward
- ⓛ smile
- ⓜ look away
- ⓝ impress the other person
- ⓞ line up your shoulders
- ⓟ move in the same way

MEN	MEN AND WOMEN	WOMEN

UNIT 2

ENGLISH AS A GLOBAL LANGUAGE

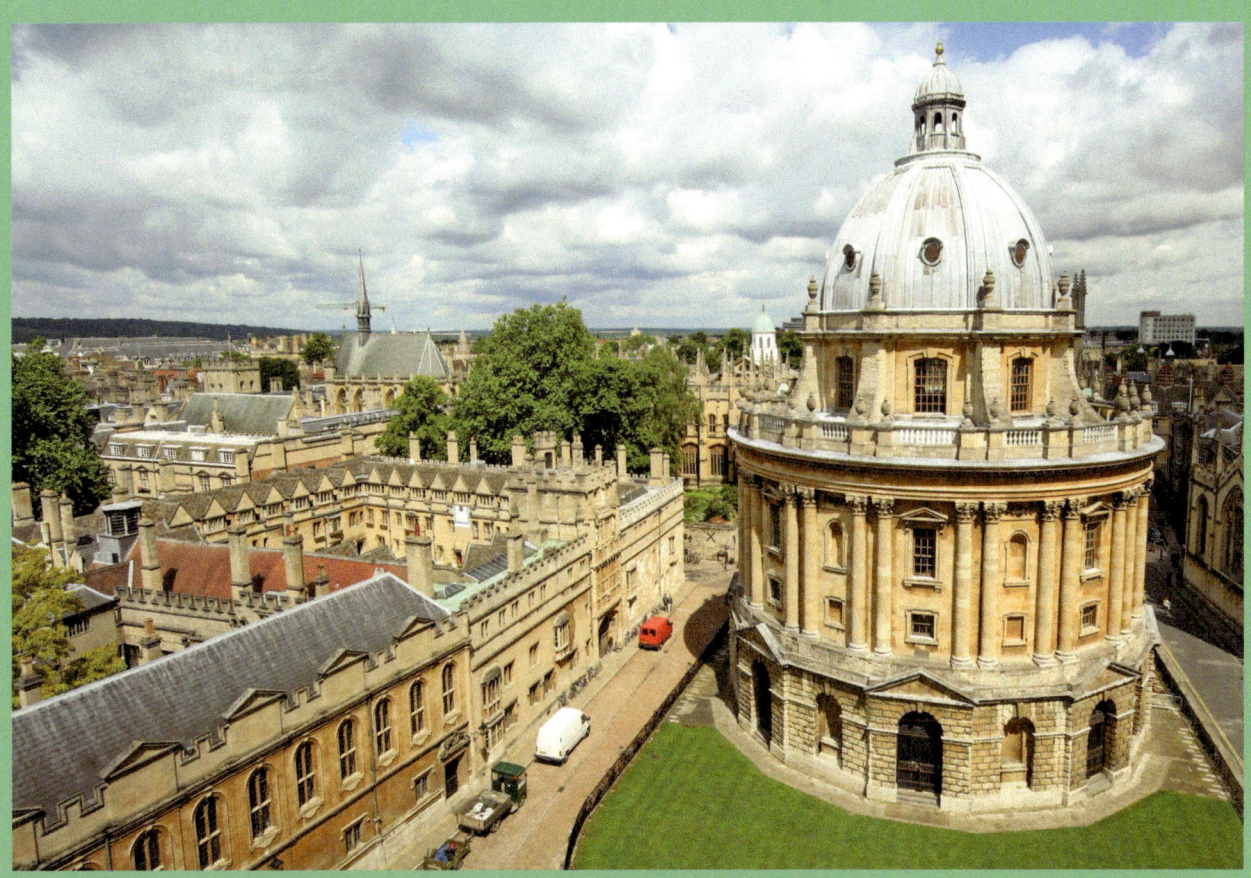

Lesson 3. The Changing World of English
Focused Reading The Rise of English in the World
Reinforcement Reading Language and Power

Lesson 4. World Englishes and English Worlds
Focused Reading The Emergence of New Varieties of English
Reinforcement Reading Different Purposes of Learning English

UNIT 2

LESSON 3.
The Changing World of English

■ **PRE-DISCUSSION FOCUS**

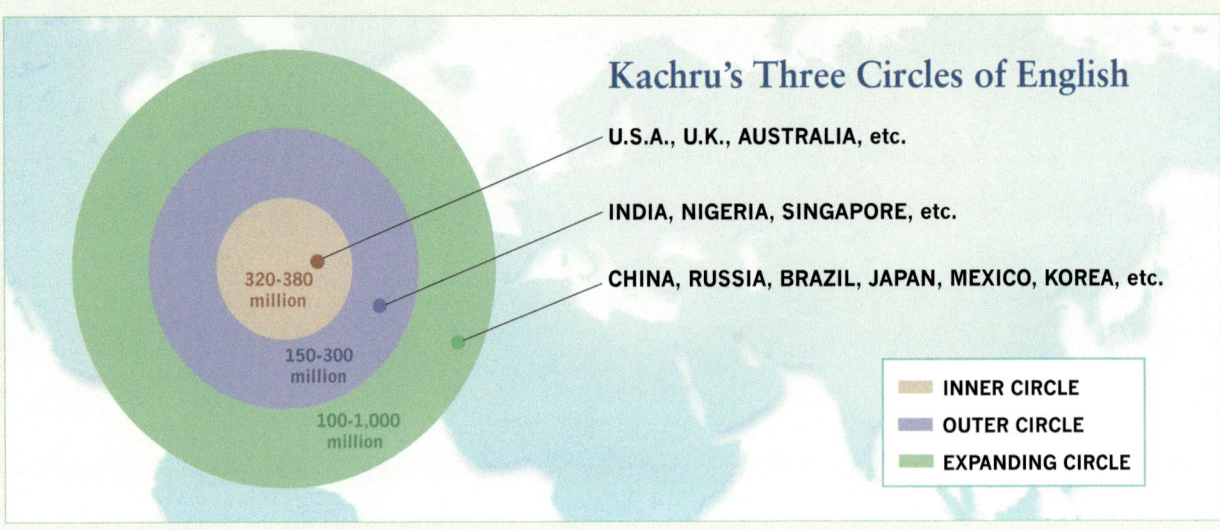

1. Why do you think Kachru made the three concentric circles of English?
   ....

2. List the five most popular languages in the world. Compare your list with your partner's list.

MY LIST	MY PARTNER'S LIST

■ **SCHEMA FOCUS**

Read the statements below and write **T** for true, **F** for false or **NS** for what you are not sure of.

1. There is only one correct form of English. ....
2. Nearly one quarter of people on earth today can use English well. ....
3. America is the reason why English is such a powerful language in the world. ....
4. English has always been the international language. ....
5. The English used in the countries making up the three circles of English is very different. ....
   People from one circle have difficulty understanding people from other circles.

32 UNIT 2

The Rise of English in the World

These days, it seems clear that everyone can **communicate in** English. English is truly becoming an international language. It is easy to find people who have a very good **command** of English in almost every country in the world. There are many popular languages around the world, but none of them are as dominant as English. English is becoming more **influential** every year. This simple fact is changing many things around the world.

English has not always been a significant language. Until the end of the 15th century, it **was confined to** England, but as the British Empire expanded over the following 500 years, English's influence grew dramatically. At one point, England controlled the largest empire in history. After two World Wars and the Cold War, it was a former British colony, the United States, which **emerged** as the new superpower. People in this country also spoke English and so English's **dominance** continues to this day with America as the global power. Someday English may be less important, but for now, it is the language that allows people to communicate successfully in most countries around the world. The fact is that English is becoming a global language.

There has never been a global language before, so people are not sure what will happen if it occurs. Historically, Latin was the most influential international language. It was used throughout the Roman Empire. For a while, people in almost all of Europe spoke Latin. It was also spoken in parts of Asia and Africa. Over time, Latin changed into different languages including French and Spanish. Today, almost one billion people around the world speak these languages. English does not come from Latin, but it still uses the Latin alphabet. Clearly, the **effects** of Latin are still important.

English is now spoken in a much larger area and has many more speakers than Latin ever did. Almost **one fourth** of the world's population living today can communicate in English well. The effects of English will probably be much larger than the effects of Latin. English already has worldwide effects in almost every area of life.

English is often used for politics. Just 150 years ago, most international leaders spoke French when they met. Now, they speak

HUMANITIES
Linguistics

English. English is the first language of many international groups including the United Nations. With England and America having been the dominant powers of the last 500 years and holding 2 of the 5 **permanent** seats in the UN, it is easy to see why their language has become so dominant.

Most scientists and researchers publish their research in English. There is some research in other languages, but almost ninety percent of all research papers are published in English. This makes it very difficult for a student to succeed without knowing English.

Many of the world's most famous newspapers, such as The New York Times, are published in English. Hollywood and Bollywood movies are produced in English. Many of the world's most popular songs are written in English. Airplane pilots must learn to speak English well before they are allowed to fly internationally. The list of reasons why English is important **never seems to end**.

This situation will have an effect on English because most of the people now speaking English are not native English speakers. They learned English at school, not as children at home. In 1985, Kachru described the world of English in terms of three concentric circles. The smallest circle was the inner circle. This circle included native English speakers from countries like the U.S., the U.K. and Australia where English is the primary language. It had only between 300 and 400 million speakers. The outer circle had a similar number of speakers. This circle included countries that used English as a Second Language (ESL). These were countries like India and Singapore. The third circle was the **expanding** circle. It included almost a billion people. These were people from countries that study **English as a Foreign Language (EFL)**, like Korea, Japan and China.

There is no question that English is strong today. It is much harder to say what will happen in the future. Individual attitudes, international politics and many other factors will go into determining the future of English. Experts agree that English will continue to become more popular for a while. Over the next few years, English will grow. Even more people will learn to speak English. English will be used even more often in meetings around the world. After that, **it's anyone's guess**.

1 Basic Skills Focus

■ RECALL FACTS

1. What two countries are mainly responsible for English's power these days?
   Write the number "1" in the passage.

2. What language was most widely spoken in Europe before English according to the passage?
   Write the number "2" in the passage.

3. What was the international language of politics immediately before English?
   Write the number "3" in the passage.

4. What is English being used for around the globe these days? Write the number "4" in the passage.

5. What are the three circles of English? Write the number "5" in the passage.

■ IDENTIFY FACTS

1. What was the international language of politics right before English?
   a. Latin
   b. Chinese
   c. French
   d. Spanish

2. Which of the following is **NOT** a reason for English becoming a global language?
   a. It is the language of aviation.
   b. Many movies and songs are in English.
   c. Most scientists use English in their papers.
   d. There are many more native speakers than non-native speakers.

3. Which of the following is **NOT** one of the three circles of English?
   a. the small circle
   b. the inner circle
   c. the outer circle
   d. the expanding circle

4. In which language is most research done these days?
   a. Latin
   b. English
   c. French
   d. Spanish

5. Which of the following is true?
   a. The inner and outer circles of English have about the same number of speakers.
   b. English will continue to get more popular until everyone speaks it.
   c. Everyone learns to speak the same English.
   d. Latin was the first global language.

LESSON 3 The Changing World of English

2 Reading Skills Focus

■ MAIN IDEA

1. What is the main idea of the reading?

    a. a discussion of English as a global language

    b. a discussion of English as the best international language

    c. a history of the Latin and English languages

■ AUTHOR'S PURPOSE

1. The author wrote this article to ....

    a. explain why English is the easiest language to learn

    b. talk about the state of English as a world language now

    c. explain how many people speak English and where they live

■ DETAIL

1. What was the most powerful language in history before English?

    a. French

    b. Spanish

    c. Latin

■ INFERENCE

1. What can be inferred from the passage?

    a. English will become more complex as more people begin to speak it.

    b. English will continue to become more popular for at least a few more years.

    c. English will not change much in the future because everyone will learn it perfectly.

2. What can we learn from the fact that Latin and English have been two of the most dominant languages in history?

    a. Both political and military power give a language power.

    b. Latin and English are the two best languages in the world.

    c. English will eventually be forgotten, just like Latin.

■ CONTEXT CLUE

| permanent | command | EFL | expanding | dominance |

1. .... is the study of English by non-native speakers living in a non-English speaking environment.

2. The .... number of people who study English proves that English is used internationally to communicate with one another.

3. When you speak English fluently, it means you have a good .... of English.

4. England used to control the seas, and because of its .... on the water, it was able to build a huge empire.

5. If certain countries are always part of the UN Security Council, they are its .... members.

36 UNIT 2

3 Thinking Skills Focus

■ PARAPHRASING SKILLS

1. This circle included native English speakers from countries like the U.S., the U.K. and Australia.

    a. The U.S., U.K. and Australia are the inner circle.
    b. The U.S., U.K. and Australia are part of the inner circle.
    c. Native speakers from the U.S., U.K. and Australia live in the inner circle.

2. The list of reasons why English is important never seems to end.

    a. There are many reasons why English is important.
    b. The reasons why English is important will end.
    c. It seems that the English list is very long.

■ CRITICAL THINKING SKILLS

1. Which of the following is **NOT** a reason why you should study English?

    a. to watch foreign films
    b. to be included in the inner circle
    c. to understand new research

2. The United States took control of the Philippines from Spain in 1898. Since that time, English has become something of a second language for people there. It helps the people on all the different islands, many of whom have very different languages, to communicate. It is taught in school and used in some jobs. Where would Kachru place the Philippines in his circles of English?

    a. inner circle of English
    b. outer circle of English
    c. expanding circle of English

■ LOGICAL REASONING SKILLS

Read the paragraph below. Then, insert the sentence in the box into the passage at one of the numbered sites by checking the appropriate number.

English is now more powerful and more widespread than Latin ever was.

   Historically, Latin was the most powerful language. ① It gave us the Romance languages like French and Spanish. ② While English does not come from Latin, it uses the Latin alphabet. ③ It is used in many fields around the world and is the most common second language taught in schools. ④ The number of English learners in the expanding circle is increasing rapidly.

LESSON 3 The Changing World of English

4 Language Skills Focus

■ **VOCABULARY DEFINITION**

1. If England is a(n) .... country, they can force other countries to do what they want them to do.
   a. permanent
   b. influential

2. While Latin may have died as a language, we can still see the .... it had on the world in the form of the Roman alphabet and the Romance languages.
   a. effects
   b. factors

3. For a long time, English was only spoken in England, so it was .... to one island.
   a. confined
   b. dominated

4. As the strength of the British Empire began to fall, the U.S. .... as a global force.
   a. occurred
   b. emerged

■ **LANGUAGE FORMS**

1. The people of the world .... English. They speak and write one another in English.
   a. communicate by
   b. communicate with
   c. communicate for
   d. communicate in

2. English replaced Latin as the most powerful language in the world. Nearly .... of people on earth today can use English well.
   a. one forth
   b. one forths
   c. one fourth
   d. one fourths

3. The number of reasons for learning English ....
   a. seems never to end
   b. never seems to end
   c. seem never to end
   d. never seem to end

4. No one knows what the future of the English language will be. ....
   a. Its anyone's guess
   b. Its anyone guess
   c. It's anyone's guess
   d. It's anyone guess

5 Structure Skills Focus

■ REFERENT IDENTIFICATION

English is truly becoming an international language. It is easy to find people who have a very good command of English in almost every country in the world. There are many popular languages around the world, but none of **them** are as dominant as English.

1. What does "them" refer to?

 a. people

 b. almost every country

 c. many popular languages

England controlled the largest empire in history. After two World Wars and the Cold War, it was a former British colony, the United States, which emerged as the new superpower. People in **this country** also spoke English and so English's dominance continues to this day with America as the global power.

2. What does "this country" refer to?

 a. England

 b. the United States

 c. the largest empire

■ ERROR CORRECTION

1. The inner circle <u>of</u> English contains <u>less</u> people <u>than</u> any other <u>circle</u>.
　　　　　　　ⓐ　　　　　　　　ⓑ　　　　　ⓒ　　　　　　　ⓓ

2. <u>There</u> are many popular <u>language</u> <u>around</u> <u>the</u> world.
　　ⓐ　　　　　　　　　　ⓑ　　　　ⓒ　　ⓓ

3. <u>It</u> <u>seems</u> <u>clearly</u> that English is <u>becoming</u> more important.
　　ⓐ　ⓑ　　ⓒ　　　　　　　　　ⓓ

4. Latin was the <u>dominantest</u> international language, and <u>it</u> was used <u>throughout</u>
　　　　　　　　ⓐ　　　　　　　　　　　　　　　　ⓑ　　　　　　ⓒ
the Roman <u>Empire</u>.
　　　　　ⓓ

5. English already has <u>worldwide</u> <u>effects</u> in <u>most</u> every area <u>of</u> life.
　　　　　　　　　　　ⓐ　　　　ⓑ　　　ⓒ　　　　　　ⓓ

6. <u>In</u> the next five <u>years</u>, millions more people <u>have</u> learn <u>to</u> speak English.
　　ⓐ　　　　　　　ⓑ　　　　　　　　　　　　ⓒ　　　　ⓓ

7. <u>None</u> of <u>them</u> are <u>as</u> <u>dominantly</u> as English.
　　ⓐ　　　ⓑ　　　ⓒ　　ⓓ

8. Almost ninety <u>percents</u> of all research <u>papers</u> are <u>published</u> <u>in</u> English.
　　　　　　　ⓐ　　　　　　　　　　ⓑ　　　　ⓒ　　　ⓓ

9. About one <u>forth</u> of the <u>world's</u> population can communicate most <u>in</u> English
　　　　　　ⓐ　　　　　ⓑ　　　　　　　　　　　　　　　　　　ⓒ
<u>properly</u>.
　ⓓ

10. <u>All</u> international airline pilots <u>must</u> have a good <u>command</u> <u>with</u> English.
　　ⓐ　　　　　　　　　　　　ⓑ　　　　　　　　ⓒ　　ⓓ

6 Communication Skills Focus

■ **ACCURACY SKILLS**

Answer the following questions by writing full sentences. Use the clues to help you come up with the correct answer.

1. Where was Latin spoken when it was most dominant?
   • Europe • Asia and Africa

   ....

2. What percentage of research papers are published in English?
   • almost • percent of

   ....

■ **FLUENCY SKILLS**

Discuss your answers with a partner. Use the clues to help you come up with the correct answer.

1. What does it mean to be a non-native speaker of English?
   • study • instead of

2. What classification system did Kachru invent?
   • concentric • classify

■ **PERSONALIZING SKILLS**

Answer the following questions with your own ideas in full sentences.

1. How and where does English affect your life?

2. Do you think English will be more or less powerful in the future? Why?

Reinforcement Reading

Read the short passage below that expands on the reading at the beginning of the lesson. Then, cross out the unnecessary sentence by checking the box next to it.

France conquered England in the year 1066. ☐ After that, French became the language of the higher classes in England. ☐ It was only the poor people who spoke English, and even they adopted many French words. ☐ People were also eager to speak Spanish. Many years later, it was England that was strong. The English explored the world and conquered many people. ☐ English became a dominant language in such far away places as India, Hong Kong and the United States.

Language and Power

7 Presentation Skills Focus

■ Give a presentation using a visual aid.

STEP 1 PLAN
Fill in the diagram using specific details from Kachru's Three Circles of English. First, fill in the missing information on the x-axis. Next, draw an appropriately sized bar for each of the circles of English. How many people are there in each of the circles of English? Then, write the names of 2 to 3 countries from each circle inside the appropriate bar. Shade in the bar that represents your home country. Finally, review the content in the main reading and plan your presentation.

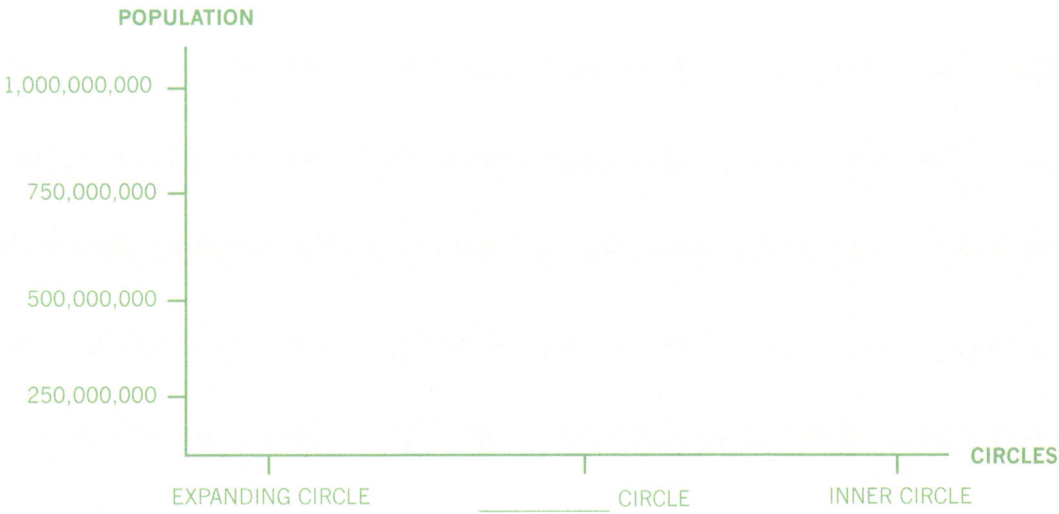

STEP 2 PREPARE
Use the "Outline" chart below to prepare your presentation about "Kachru's Model of the Three Circles and Its Implications." You may prepare an outline by making some notes in the space below.

OUTLINE		
1. Introduction	**2. Body**	**3. Conclusion**

• Attention Getter/Hook
• Statement of Topic
• Overview
  - Main Point 1
  - Main Point 2
  - Main Point 3
	• Main Point 1
	  - Examples/Evidence
	• Main Point 2
	  - Examples/Evidence
	• Main Point 3
	  - Examples/Evidence
		• Restatement of Topic
		• Main Point 1
		  - Brief Review
		• Main Point 2
		  - Brief Review
		• Main Point 3
		  - Brief Review
		• Closing Comment

STEP 3 PRACTICE
Pair up. Then, deliver your presentation to each other.

STEP 4 PERFORM
Present your completed presentation to the class. Then, complete the peer evaluation record using a scale from 1 (lowest) to 5 (highest).

PEER EVALUATION RECORD
Presenter's Name: ....

Delivery	Grade				
Posture	1	2	3	4	5
Eye Contact	1	2	3	4	5
Gestures	1	2	3	4	5
Voice Inflection	1	2	3	4	5
Content	**Grade**				
Introduction	1	2	3	4	5
Body	1	2	3	4	5
Use of Evidence	1	2	3	4	5
Conclusion	1	2	3	4	5

UNIT 2

LESSON 4.
World Englishes and English Worlds

■ **PRE-DISCUSSION FOCUS**

1. Can you name some countries where English is spoken as a second language? Do they speak English in the same way? Discuss your answers.

   ....

2. How many different types of English can you think of? List them and compare your list to your partner's.

MY LIST	MY PARTNER'S LIST
e.g. Singlish	

■ **SCHEMA FOCUS**

Read the statements below and write **T** for true, **F** for false or **NS** for what you are not sure of.

1. There are as many world Englishes as there are native English speaking countries. ....
2. If you are going to study a language, your goal doesn't have to be to learn it perfectly. ....
3. Experts know what the future of English will be. ....
4. Most of the people who speak English these days are non-native speakers. ....
5. English can be made simpler so that more people can understand it. ....

The Emergence of New Varieties of English

World Englishes are localized varieties of English often spoken in areas **colonized** or under the influence of England or the U.S. With the spread of English continuing to grow, there are many more non-native speakers starting to speak the language. These people come from many different language backgrounds, so they use and change English in many different ways.

For many years, people in countries like Korea and Japan have taught English as a Foreign Language (EFL). Students needed to learn "correct" English to pass tests and to **succeed in** school and business. Other people learning English expected to use it for traveling or doing business in English-speaking countries. They learned English so that they could communicate with native English speakers. Generally, either American or British English was taught.

Today, this is changing somewhat, and some people are starting to teach **English as an International Language (EIL)**. Because there are so many non-native speakers now, people usually use English with other people for whom English is a second or **foreign** language. Many people rarely speak English to native English speakers.

The increase in non-native speakers has changed the way English is taught in the classroom, which has led many teachers and students to believe they need to learn a different kind of English. **Instead of** learning to speak "perfect" English, students should learn to communicate competently in English. They say that students do not have to speak like people in the U.S. or the U.K. It is more important to speak clearly so that anyone can understand. This means that English is often used **in a simplified way**.

What English is best for you to learn no doubt **depends upon** your goals. Students who plan to study abroad in an English-speaking country probably need to learn very correct English. These students can only reach their goals if they can use English correctly. Other students, who in their careers will never or very rarely **interact with** native speakers, may use English in different ways. For them, it may be better to **focus on** using English to communicate ideas with other non-native speakers.

HUMANITIES
Linguistics

Some of these people even say that native speakers are not very good at communicating with non-native speakers. Native speakers should be more patient and try harder to speak clearly and **comprehensibly**. This international language is something different from English in the U.S. or the U.K., and native English speakers should learn to speak this international English. They should learn to simplify their speech so that everyone can understand.

Over the next few years, many more people will learn English, but no one knows what will happen after that. As the world changes, languages will change, too. After many years, one of three things will probably happen. First, people in some countries might stop using English. They might feel that English is being overused and making their culture **vanish** slowly. If they start to feel that way, they will not want to use English. Then, English could become less influential around the world, and another language could become more prevalent.

Another possibility is that English could **split into** many separate languages. This will not happen soon, but it is not unlikely. English is already different in different places. People in different countries change English to make it work in their cultures. They add words from their own language, and they use grammar in new ways. English in the U.K. is similar to English in the U.S., but it is not the same. English in Singapore is even more different. In fact, in Singapore, many people use a language that is a form of English with Chinese and Malay influences. They call it Singlish. Singlish is an example of a world English. It uses some words that are not English, and its grammar is often different from the grammar of most other Englishes. If people in different countries continue to talk to each other, English will not split. However, these people may also all use slightly different variations of English in their own countries or regions.

Finally, English could become even more prevalent. When a language becomes too dominant, people only learn one language and stop learning other languages. At some point, this might cause other languages to **die out**.

It is hard to predict what will happen to English. However, English is likely to be the first language to become a truly global language. It could be that in a few more years, almost everyone in the world will be able to speak English. If that happens, we will all have to decide what kind of English we want to speak.

*Malay: a language spoken in Malaysia

1 Basic Skills Focus

■ RECALL FACTS

1. Why is EIL becoming more popular? Write the number "1" in the passage.

2. Why would some students want to learn more "correct" forms of English? Write the number "2" in the passage.

3. What are two reasons native speakers are sometimes not very good at communicating with non-native speakers? Write the number "3" in the passage.

4. How do people change English to make it fit better with their culture and native language? Write the number "4" in the passage.

5. Which world English is mentioned in the text? Write the number "5" in the passage.

■ IDENTIFY FACTS

1. Which of the following is **NOT** a possible future for English?
    a. English will become more prevalent.
    b. English will split into various languages.
    c. English will become less prevalent.
    d. English will stop changing.

2. For many years, what particular kind of English has been taught in Korean classrooms?
    a. EIL
    b. EFL
    c. Konglish
    d. Singlish

3. Which of the following would be a situation in which people may stop using English?
    a. if people feel their culture is disappearing because of English
    b. if people feel their culture is splitting because of English
    c. if people feel their culture is becoming more prevalent because of English
    d. if people feel their culture is globalizing because of English

4. What is **NOT** a possible consequence of English becoming too influential?
    a. speak only English
    b. split into many separate languages
    c. overuse English and stop learning it
    d. create a new language

5. Which of the following is **NOT** a part of Singlish?
    a. Chinese
    b. French
    c. Malay
    d. English

2 Reading Skills Focus

■ MAIN IDEA

1. What is the main idea of the reading?
    a. the exploration of world Englishes with three possible futures
    b. the importance of learning to speak standard North American English
    c. how to simplify the English language

■ AUTHOR'S PURPOSE

1. The author wrote this article to ....
    a. inform the audience about how English can be taught and talk about its past
    b. inform the audience about how English can be taught and what its future may be
    c. explain how to teach English

■ DETAIL

1. What is the main goal of English as an International Language?
    a. to have a non-native English speaking teacher
    b. to speak clearly so that anyone can understand
    c. to be able to communicate clearly with native speakers

■ INFERENCE

1. Why are more countries and schools teaching English as an International Language these days?
    a. Because English is impossible to learn perfectly.
    b. Because teaching English as a Foreign Language has been proven to be ineffective.
    c. Because there are so many non-native English speakers, and they need to be able to speak clearly rather than speak perfectly.

2. What could happen to English in different countries if people no longer interact with foreigners?
    a. English could split into a number of new and different languages.
    b. It could kill off many other languages.
    c. English could become much more similar around the world.

■ CONTEXT CLUE

| foreign | depends upon | colonized | EIL | comprehensibly |

1. The type of English people need to study .... the purpose of their learning.

2. Non-native speakers tend to learn .... as they rarely have to interact with native speakers.

3. English in .... areas has always been a little bit different from standard English.

4. Native English speakers should try hard to speak .... so that non-native speakers easily undertand them.

5. Many people in the world have to learn English because it is not their mother tongue but a .... language.

3 Thinking Skills Focus

■ PARAPHRASING SKILLS

1. In fact, in Singapore, many people use a language that is a form of English with Chinese and Malay influences.

   a. People in Singapore cannot speak Chinese or Malay, only a new version of English.
   b. Singaporean English contains some Chinese and some Malay.
   c. Chinese and Malay have influenced English.

2. The increase in non-native speakers has changed the way English is taught in the classroom.

   a. Non-native teachers are finally teaching English in classrooms.
   b. More non-native speakers are learning English in classrooms.
   c. English is being taught differently because there are more non-native speakers.

■ CRITICAL THINKING SKILLS

1. What is the most likely consequence of more people learning English as an International Language?
   a. More people will speak perfect English.
   b. English will become simpler and less like "standard" English.
   c. Fewer people will be able to communicate with native speakers.

2. In the past, Latin split into many different languages. Some people think that the same thing is happening to English and that it will become a number of different languages. Which of the following is an example of this?
   a. people in Singapore speaking Singlish
   b. British people learning American English from movies and TV
   c. English becoming a global language

■ LOGICAL REASONING SKILLS

Read the paragraph below. Then, insert the sentence in the box into the passage at one of the numbered sites by checking the appropriate number.

Others prefer to try and learn "perfect" English.

The increase in English as a Second Language speakers means that both English and the way it is taught are changing. ① Some people believe English should be taught in a simplified form to be more useful as an international language between two non-native speakers. ② The type of English people choose to learn and speak will determine the future of the language. ③ It could become less popular if people begin to reject it. ④ It could split into different languages or it could become even more popular and influential.

4 Language Skills Focus

■ VOCABULARY DEFINITION

1. Many native languages have .... slowly after their lands have been colonized. The languages do not exist anymore.

    a. vanished
    b. overused

2. Latin .... many languages. Spanish, French, Italian and Portuguese all come from Latin.

    a. separated
    b. split into

3. Some native speakers tend to speak English in a .... way to communicate more easily with non-native speakers.

    a. localized
    b. simplified

4. If you .... a native speaker, you listen and speak with them to communicate.

    a. interact with
    b. succeed in

■ LANGUAGE FORMS

1. Most non-native English speakers need to learn English to .... achieving their academic and professional goals.

    a. succeed for
    b. success for
    c. succeed in
    d. success in

2. .... American English, why don't we try speaking British English today?

    a. Instead
    b. Instead of
    c. Instead for
    d. In instead for

3. The aim of EIL classes is .... the ability to communicate clearly and simply.

    a. to focus on
    b. to focus of
    c. to focusing on
    d. to focusing of

4. The popularity of English might cause some other languages ....

    a. dying off
    b. to die off
    c. dying out
    d. to die out

5 Structure Skills Focus

▪ REFERENT IDENTIFICATION

Another possibility is that English could split into many separate languages. This will not happen soon, but <u>it</u> is not unlikely. English is already different in different places.

1. What does "it" refer to?
   a. the English language
   b. the splitting of English
   c. happening soon

English in the U.K. is similar to English in the U.S., but it is not the same. English in Singapore is even more different. In fact, in Singapore, many people use a language that is a form of English with Chinese and Malay influences. They call it Singlish. Singlish is an example of a world English. It uses some words that are not English, and <u>its</u> grammar is often different from the grammar of most other Englishes.

2. What does "its" refer to?
   a. Singapore
   b. Singlish
   c. Malay

▪ ERROR CORRECTION

1. People <u>learning</u> English as <u>Foreign</u> Language are expected <u>to</u> speak <u>with</u> native speakers.
   (a)   (b)   (c)   (d)

2. Foreign language <u>learners</u> <u>want</u> <u>to</u> communicate <u>in</u> native speakers.
                    (a)   (b)   (c)   (d)

3. <u>Students</u> do <u>not</u> have to speak <u>alike</u> people in <u>the</u> U.S. or U.K.
   (a)   (b)   (c)   (d)

4. Instead <u>to</u> learning <u>to</u> speak "perfect" English, <u>they</u> should just learn <u>to</u> communicate.
           (a)   (b)   (c)   (d)

5. <u>There</u> <u>are</u> people <u>with</u> many different <u>languages</u> backgrounds in the U.S.
   (a)   (b)   (c)   (d)

6. <u>Many</u> people in <u>colony</u> areas <u>learned</u> <u>to</u> speak English.
   (a)   (b)   (c)   (d)

7. People in <u>every</u> country change English <u>to</u> make <u>them</u> work in their <u>cultures</u>.
              (a)   (b)   (c)   (d)

8. There <u>are</u> many <u>slight</u> different <u>variations</u> of <u>Korean</u> in Korea.
         (a)   (b)   (c)   (d)

9. Have you <u>decided</u> what kind <u>of</u> English you <u>wanted</u> to <u>speak</u>?
              (a)   (b)   (c)   (d)

10. Native speakers must <u>simplify</u> <u>their</u> speech <u>such</u> that non-native speakers <u>can</u> understand.
                         (a)   (b)   (c)   (d)

LESSON 4 World Englishes and English Worlds 49

6 Communication Skills Focus

■ ACCURACY SKILLS

Answer the following questions by writing full sentences. Use the clues to help you come up with the correct answer.

1. What is EIL? To whom is it taught?
   • International • non-native speakers

   ....

2. What three things could happen to English in the future?
   • popular • split

   ....

■ FLUENCY SKILLS

Discuss your answers with a partner. Use the clues to help you come up with the correct answer.

1. Why does English get changed when it enters a new country?
   • work better • cultures

2. Why do some people think it is better to teach EIL?
   • non-native • communicate

■ PERSONALIZING SKILLS

Answer the following questions with your own ideas in full sentences.

1. What kind of English do you think you should be learning? Why?

2. What do you think will happen to the English language in the next 20 years?

Reinforcement Reading

Read the short passage below that expands on the reading at the beginning of the lesson. Then, cross out the unnecessary sentence by checking the box next to it.

An acronym is a word made from the initial letters in a group of words. There are a lot of acronyms used in the English Language Teaching (ELT) field. ☐ LOL is a new acronym, and it was invented for use in computer chats. EFL and EIL were used in the passage. ☐ ESL and ESP are other common acronyms in the field of ELT. ☐ They stand for English as a Second Language and English for Special Purposes. ☐ ESL is different from EFL in that ESL learners live in an environment where English is widely spoken. ESP is different from EGP in that ESP learners learn the language in order to communicate a set of professional skills and to perform particular-job-related functions while EGP, English for General Purposes, learners study the language to improve their everyday communication skills.

Different Purposes of Learning English

50 UNIT 2

7 Presentation Skills Focus

■ Give a presentation using a visual aid.

STEP 1 PLAN

Fill in the chart using specific details from the passage of the lesson. First, write all the advantages of English becoming a global language on the left side. Next, write all the disadvantages on the right side. Then, write anything you are unsure about or that is neutral in the middle.

ADVANTAGES	NEUTRAL	DISADVANTAGES

STEP 2 PREPARE

Use the "Outline" chart below to prepare your presentation about "English as a Global Language, a Good Thing or Bad Thing?" You may prepare an outline by making some notes in the space below.

OUTLINE		
1. Introduction	**2. Body**	**3. Conclusion**

• Attention Getter/Hook
• Statement of Topic
• Overview
  · Main Point 1
  · Main Point 2
  · Main Point 3
	• Main Point 1
	  · Examples/Evidence
	• Main Point 2
	  · Examples/Evidence
	• Main Point 3
	  · Examples/Evidence
		• Restatement of Topic
		• Main Point 1
		  · Brief Review
		• Main Point 2
		  · Brief Review
		• Main Point 3
		  · Brief Review
		• Closing Comment

STEP 3 PRACTICE

Pair up. Then, deliver your presentation to each other.

STEP 4 PERFORM

Present your completed presentation to the class. Then, complete the peer evaluation record using a scale from 1 (lowest) to 5 (highest).

PEER EVALUATION RECORD

Presenter's Name: ....

Delivery	Grade				
Posture	1	2	3	4	5
Eye Contact	1	2	3	4	5
Gestures	1	2	3	4	5
Voice Inflection	1	2	3	4	5
Content	**Grade**				
Introduction	1	2	3	4	5
Body	1	2	3	4	5
Use of Evidence	1	2	3	4	5
Conclusion	1	2	3	4	5

UNIT 2 REVIEW

INFORMATION ORGANIZATION

Fill in the graphic organizer with details from the passages you have read.

LANGUAGE TIMELINE

PAST
- .... was the most dominant language in history
- Latin was spoken in ....
- Latin split into .... and ....,
  and it also gave English its alphabet

↓

- for a time, after Latin's importance had dropped, ...
  was the international language of politics

↓

PRESENT
- the fact that research, ..., ...,
  ...., politics and airline .... use English
  as the international language shows how influential English is in the world today
- → it really is the .... language

↓

- because English is an international language, some people think it should be taught as
  such → English is now used more often by ....
  to talk to other non-native speakers, rather than to talk to native speakers
- → this is changing the language

↙ ↓ ↘

POSSIBLE FUTURE

FUTURE 1	FUTURE 2	FUTURE 3
....	....	....
....	....	....
....	....	....
....	....	....

SOCIAL SCIENCES
Sociology

UNIT 3

HUMAN RIGHTS

Lesson 5. The Basics of Human Rights

Focused Reading Fundamental Human Rights and the United Nations
Reinforcement Reading The Magna Carta: The Cornerstone of Human Rights

Lesson 4. The History of Human Rights

Focused Reading The Origins of Ideas about Human Rights
Reinforcement Reading Mahatma Gandhi: Champion of Human Rights

UNIT 3

LESSON 5.
The Basics of Human Rights

■ **PRE-DISCUSSION FOCUS**

1. What basic human rights do you know?

2. Why are human rights important? Discuss your answer with a partner.

MY OPINION	MY PARTNER'S OPINION

■ **SCHEMA FOCUS**

Read the statements below and write **T** for true, **F** for false or **NS** for what you are not sure of.

1. Everyone believes all people should be treated with respect.
2. The Universal Declaration of Human Rights is an international law.
3. It is easy to protect civil and political rights.
4. The United States does not guarantee all its people economic, social and cultural rights.
5. The UN Covenant on Civil and Political Rights has less international support than the Universal Declaration of Human Rights.

Fundamental Human Rights and the United Nations

Today, most people believe that every human being should be **treated** with respect. They believe that every person in the world has certain rights simply because they are human. It is difficult to be certain that everyone is getting these rights. In today's world, the fact that governments can be very embarrassed if they do not give their people their basic rights, helps to maintain a certain standard of **dignity** across the world.

There are two main categories of human rights in the world today: civil and political rights and economic, social and cultural rights.

Civil and political rights are about people and their relationship to the government. For example, **the right to** a fair trial is about people's relationship to the government. People should not be punished unless they really did something wrong. Also, the right to express any political opinion is a civil right. People can share their ideas freely. People also have the right to be treated well even if they are of a different age or from a different culture.

Civil and political rights can easily be protected. Governments do not have to do anything special to protect these rights. In fact, people only lose these rights when governments do something to **take** them **away**. It is easy for people to see if a country lets its people have these rights. Sometimes, if governments take these rights away, people can even go to court to **demand** them back. Special international courts make this possible in difficult situations.

The other type of human rights is economic, social and cultural rights. These rights outline how people relate to their society and culture. An example of an economic right is the right to housing. No one should have to **live on the street**. People also have the right to get a basic education and the right to see a doctor if they are sick. With these rights, people can live a happy life.

Economic, social and cultural rights are much more difficult to see and judge than civil and political rights. Governments often set up special programs to protect people's economic, social and cultural rights. It can be very expensive for governments to **make sure** that everyone has a place to live or to make sure that everyone can see a doctor. It also takes a lot of time to make sure that everyone has these rights.

Many countries do not give their people all of these rights. For example, in the United States, many people cannot see a doctor if they are sick because

SOCIAL SCIENCES
Sociology

35 they do not have any health insurance.

Every kind of human right is important. It is not possible to truly have civil and political rights without economic, social and cultural rights. Without civil and political rights, it is impossible to ask for economic, social and cultural rights. People have to be able to communicate with their government before
40 they can ask for education or housing. Also, if people cannot read because they did not get an education, they will not be able to vote for political leaders. Choosing political leaders is an important political right.

Many people say that everyone **deserves** all the rights discussed above because all people are people. They say that people everywhere are the same
45 inside, so their rights do not change. Other people say that rights should be different in different places. Some cultures **value** certain ideas more than others, and there may be some ideas that they do not value at all. In that case, some people say that they do not need to be given those rights.

Today, all people have certain rights **guaranteed** by the United Nations
50 (UN). The Universal **Declaration** of Human Rights was written in 1948, after World War II, when people were determined never to allow such a terrible event to happen again. The declaration is not law, but it is so important that most of the rights it grants have now been **adopted** as law by most countries. This means that people respect it as law. The majority of countries in the
55 world try to provide their people the rights granted in the United Nations' Universal Declaration of Human Rights. Since 1976, the UN **Covenant** on Civil and Political Rights has been international law. This means that people can go to the International Court of Justice if they do not have civil and political rights in their country. The UN can make countries give their citizens these rights.

60 The UN has also made covenants about several other human rights. There is a covenant about how soldiers can be treated. Another covenant says that governments cannot kill people because of their culture. Also, governments cannot cause anyone to suffer from too much pain, and they cannot force women or children to live very uncomfortable lives. There is even a Covenant
65 on Economic, Social and Cultural Rights. However, not enough countries have agreed to these covenants, and they are not yet international law.

The UN has an organization called the Human Rights Council. The Human Rights Council tries to make sure that everyone in the world has human rights. It does research around the world to find out which countries do not allow
70 their people basic human rights. Then, it demands that these governments give their people their rights. If they do not, the United Nations might punish them economically, or it might ask the International Court of Justice to make a decision about the country.

1 Basic Skills Focus

■ RECALL FACTS

1. What is it that helps to maintain a certain standard of dignity across the world in terms of human rights? Write the number "1" in the passage.

2. Are economic, social and cultural rights easy for governments to grant their citizens? Write the number "2" in the passage.

3. Can you have one type of human right without the others? Write the number "3" in the passage.

4. Does everyone agree that all people deserve and need all the same rights? Write the number "4" in the passage.

5. What does the UN Covenant on Civil and Political Rights allow people to do? Write the number "5" in the passage.

■ IDENTIFY FACTS

1. Which of the following is **NOT** a basic human right?
    a. the right to housing
    b. the right to work at the UN
    c. the right to vote
    d. the right to a fair trial

2. Which of the following is **NOT** true of civil and political rights?
    a. These rights are easy to protect.
    b. They are about people's relationship to the government.
    c. They give you the right to express any political opinion you like.
    d. They include the right to a basic education.

3. Which of the following is **NOT** true of economic, social and cultural rights?
    a. They allow people to lead a happy life.
    b. They include the right to see a doctor when you are sick.
    c. They do not exist in the United States.
    d. They can be very expensive and time-consuming.

4. Which of the following is **NOT** part of the UN Covenant on Civil and Political Rights?
    a. It explains how soldiers can be treated.
    b. It allows people to go to an international court to find justice.
    c. It has been international law since 1976.
    d. It forces countries to give their people civil and political rights.

5. Which of the following is the right to see a doctor when you are sick?
    a. political
    b. economic and social
    c. cultural
    d. civil

LESSON 5 The Basics of Human Rights 57

2 Reading Skills Focus

■ MAIN IDEA

1. What is the main idea of the reading?
    a. how the UN has introduced human rights around the world
    b. an introduction to different human rights
    c. the Universal Declaration of Human Rights

■ AUTHOR'S PURPOSE

1. The author wrote this article to ....
    a. teach readers how the UN decides when human rights are being abused
    b. teach readers about who gets which rights
    c. teach readers about the rights all humans should receive

■ DETAIL

1. Why is **NOT** the UN Covenant on Economic, Social and Cultural Rights international law?
    a. Because not enough countries have agreed to its covenants.
    b. Because not all people have their human rights.
    c. Because the UN is not an international organization.

■ INFERENCE

1. Which of the following is **NOT** true?
    a. Without political rights, people will not have leaders.
    b. If you cannot communicate with your government, you cannot ask for housing.
    c. Not getting an education may mean you cannot read and therefore cannot vote for political leaders.

2. What can we understand happened during World War II?
    a. People learned how to make covenants.
    b. People learned what suffering was and wanted to ensure it never happened in the UN again.
    c. People suffered a lot; they lost their basic rights.

■ CONTEXT CLUE

| demand | deserve | value | Declaration | treated |

1. In Asian culture, people .... age and seniority the most. They are of great significance.

2. There is a covenant at the UN about how soldiers can be .... One of the agreements it says is that they cannot be tortured.

3. Most people believe that all people .... some basic human rights simply because we are all human.

4. The .... of Human Rights was written in 1948. It announced to the world all the basic rights to which all people were entitled.

5. Human rights are legal guarantees. People can .... them back if they are taken away.

3 Thinking Skills Focus

PARAPHRASING SKILLS

1. Governments often set up special programs to protect people's economic, social and cultural rights. It can be very expensive for governments to make sure that everyone has a place to live or to make sure that everyone can see a doctor. It also takes a lot of time to make sure that everyone has these rights.

   a. Protecting people's economic, social and cultural rights can be expensive and time-consuming for the government.
   b. Special programs ensure governments protect people's economic, social and cultural rights.
   c. It takes a lot of time and money to ensure everyone has a house and access to a doctor.

2. It is not possible to truly have civil and political rights without economic, social and cultural rights. Without civil and political rights, it is impossible to ask for economic, social and cultural rights.

   a. Economic, social and cultural rights come before civil and political rights.
   b. You cannot truly have one type of human right without the others.
   c. Civil and political rights come before economic, social and cultural rights.

CRITICAL THINKING SKILLS

1. What will happen if more countries sign the covenants on soldiers, how people should be treated and the UN Covenant on Economic, Social and Cultural Rights?

   a. The United Nations will make a declaration.
   b. They will become international law.
   c. No one will have to suffer any longer.

2. Which of the following is **NOT** a true statement?

   a. People who say everyone deserves all human rights guaranteed by the UN agree with the UN's Universal Declaration on Human Rights.
   b. People who say everyone deserves all human rights guaranteed by the UN say that it is OK for some people not to receive certain rights if they do not value them.
   c. People who believe rights should be different in different places say that cultures in different countries are very different.

LOGICAL REASONING SKILLS

Read the paragraph below. Then, insert the sentence in the box into the passage at one of the numbered sites by checking the appropriate number.

The first is the right to property and land ownership.

Economic, social and cultural human rights are all guaranteed by the Universal Declaration of Human Rights. ① We have seen what this means in general, but what does it mean specifically? ② We will look at one part of this guarantee: economic rights. There are five parts to economic rights. ③ It is possible for anyone, anywhere to buy and own land. Second is the right to fair compensation for taking property. ④ If people lose or have their property taken, they should be paid a fair price. Third, everyone has the right to a good standard of living. No one should have to live in terrible poverty. The right to decent housing is the fourth economic right. All people deserve to live in shelter capable of protecting them from their environment. Finally, we all share the right to healthcare. This includes access to doctors, hospitals and medicine.

4 Language Skills Focus

■ VOCABULARY DEFINITION

1. The UN Declaration of Human Rights is important in maintaining a standard of .... or honor across the world.

   a. dignity   b. value

2. A .... is a formal agreement between two or more people or groups. The UN has adopted a number of these agreements which set rules for how people are to be treated.

   a. declaration   b. covenant

3. The UN has .... all people certain rights. These rights must be respected by all people and governments at all times.

   a. guaranteed   b. treated

4. Many of the rights that the Universal Declaration of Human Rights grants have been .... and made into law by countries from around the world.

   a. adopted   b. taken away

■ LANGUAGE FORMS

1. The UN says that all people have .... housing, a basic education, a doctor and a vote.

   a. the right in   b. the right to
   c. the ability in   d. the ability to

2. Civil and political rights are easy to protect. In fact, they are only lost when a government decides to ....

   a. take away them   b. take out them
   c. take them away   d. take them out

3. One economic right all people have is the right not to have to .... the street, though this right is yet to be fulfilled in many places around the world.

   a. live on   b. live
   c. live by   d. living in

4. It is the job of the Human Rights Council .... everyone in the world has human rights.

   a. making sure   b. of making sure
   c. to make sure   d. make sure

5 Structure Skills Focus

■ REFERENT IDENTIFICATION

Civil and political rights can easily be protected. Governments do not have to do anything special to protect these rights. In fact, people only lose these rights when governments do something to take **them** away.

1. What does "them" refer to?
   a. people
   b. governments
   c. these rights

Many countries do not give their people all of these rights. For example, in the United States, many people cannot see a doctor if they are sick because **they** do not have any health insurance.

2. Who does "they" refer to?
   a. many countries
   b. their people
   c. many people

■ ERROR CORRECTION

1. Everyone <u>should</u> be <u>treat</u> <u>with</u> <u>respect</u>.
          (a)   (b)   (c)   (d)

2. <u>There</u> are two main <u>category</u> <u>of</u> human <u>rights</u>.
   (a)   (b)   (c)   (d)

3. People should be <u>allowed</u> <u>to share</u> their <u>opinions</u> <u>free</u>.
                  (a)   (b)   (c)   (d)

4. The UN <u>guarantees</u> economic, <u>social</u> and <u>culture</u> rights <u>to</u> all people.
           (a)   (b)   (c)   (d)

5. One right all people are <u>supposed</u> to have is the <u>right to</u> <u>choice</u> <u>their</u> political leaders.
                          (a)   (b)   (c)   (d)

6. You <u>cannot have</u> civil <u>and</u> political rights <u>without</u> economic, social and cultural <u>right</u>.
         (a)   (b)   (c)
      (d)

7. <u>Some</u> cultures <u>value</u> certain values <u>more</u> <u>then</u> others.
   (a)   (b)   (c) (d)

8. <u>The</u> Universal Declaration <u>of</u> Human Rights <u>were</u> written <u>in</u> 1948.
   (a)   (b)   (c)   (d)

9. <u>The</u> declaration is <u>no</u> law, <u>but</u> <u>it</u> is important.
   (a)   (b)   (c)(d)

10. The Human <u>Right</u> Council <u>does</u> research <u>around</u> <u>the</u> world.
                (a)   (b)   (c)   (d)

6 Communication Skills Focus

■ ACCURACY SKILLS

Answer the following questions by writing full sentences. Use the clues to help you come up with the correct answer.

1. What are the two main categories of human rights?
   • civil • economic

   ....

2. What are the two big problems governments have when maintaining economic, social and cultural rights?
   • expensive • time

   ....

■ FLUENCY SKILLS

Discuss your answers with a partner. Use the clues to help you come up with the correct answer.

1. How are all people guaranteed certain rights these days?
   • UN • Declaration

2. What did the UN Covenant on Civil and Political Rights becoming law in 1976 mean?
   • rights • International Court of Justice

■ PERSONALIZING SKILLS

Answer the following questions with your own ideas in full sentences.

1. Which rights do you think are more important: civil and political rights or economic, social and cultural rights? Why?

2. What examples do you know of where people lost their human rights? Has it happened in your country?

Reinforcement Reading

Read the short passage below that expands on the reading at the beginning of the lesson. Then, cross out the unnecessary sentence by checking the box next to it.

The Magna Carta: The Cornerstone of Human Rights

The idea of human rights is very old. It is a part of many ancient religions. It was also a part of the Magna Carta. The Magna Carta was written in 1215 in England. ☐ It put the idea that people cannot be taken to jail by the government for no reason into writing for the first time. The more modern notion that all people deserve certain rights simply because they are people originated sometime in the 1500s or 1600s. ☐ The Age of Enlightenment saw human rights become more important to scholars. The idea was behind both the American and French revolutions. ☐ As the idea continued to evolve, everyone was given the right to vote. Later human rights came to include women's rights, the civil rights of minorities and workers' rights. The two world wars finally led to the UN devising the Universal Declaration of Human Rights. ☐ Covenants have not become international law.

7 Presentation Skills Focus

■ Give a presentation using a visual aid.

STEP 1 PLAN
First, fill in the blanks to complete the chart. Next, complete the statements in the Fact File that follow based on what you've learned from the reading.

TYPES OF HUMAN RIGHTS			
TYPE ONE		EXAMPLES	
TYPE TWO		EXAMPLES	

FACT FILE

FACT 1. All people deserve human .... simply because they are ....

FACT 2. The Universal Declaration of .... was written in ....

FACT 3. The UN Covenant on .... and Political Rights became international law in ....

FACT 4. Several other covenants the UN has on human rights are ....,
....,
and ....

STEP 2 PREPARE
Use the "Outline" chart below to prepare your presentation about "The Two Types of Human Rights." You may prepare an outline by making some notes in the space below.

OUTLINE		
1. Introduction	**2. Body**	**3. Conclusion**
• Attention Getter/Hook • Statement of Topic • Overview 　· Main Point 1 　· Main Point 2 　· Main Point 3	• Main Point 1 　· Examples/Evidence • Main Point 2 　· Examples/Evidence • Main Point 3 　· Examples/Evidence	• Restatement of Topic • Main Point 1 　· Brief Review • Main Point 2 　· Brief Review • Main Point 3 　· Brief Review • Closing Comment

STEP 3 PRACTICE
Pair up. Then, deliver your presentation to each other.

STEP 4 PERFORM
Present your completed presentation to the class. Then, complete the peer evaluation record using a scale from 1 (lowest) to 5 (highest).

PEER EVALUATION RECORD
Presenter's Name: ....

Delivery	Grade				
Posture	1	2	3	4	5
Eye Contact	1	2	3	4	5
Gestures	1	2	3	4	5
Voice Inflection	1	2	3	4	5
Content	**Grade**				
Introduction	1	2	3	4	5
Body	1	2	3	4	5
Use of Evidence	1	2	3	4	5
Conclusion	1	2	3	4	5

UNIT 3

LESSON 6.
The History of Human Rights

■ **PRE-DISCUSSION FOCUS**

1. Historically, what events do you think initially led to discussions regarding the need for various categories of human rights? Give some possible examples.
   ....

2. Are there any other human rights you think all people deserve? Discuss your answer with a partner.

MY OPINION	MY PARTNER'S OPINION

■ **SCHEMA FOCUS**

Read the statements below and write **T** for true, **F** for false or **NS** for what you are not sure of.

1. Ancient Rome was the first civilization to give all its people human rights. ....
2. The King of England wrote the Magna Carta. ....
3. The destruction caused by World War II resulted in many people becoming more interested in human rights. ....
4. Gandhi freed African Americans in America. ....
5. Amnesty International is one group that works to protect human rights. ....

The Origins of Ideas about Human Rights

People have not always had human rights. For most of history, only certain people, like the rich, had human rights. In ancient Rome, only **citizens of** Rome had human rights. **None of** the slaves who lived in Rome or the people living in areas controlled by Rome had human rights.

Most people say that the first human rights were written in the Magna Carta in England in 1215. The Magna Carta limited the power of the king. It was forced on King John by his most powerful **subjects**. It stated that no freeman, that is, anyone who was not a **serf**, could be punished except through the laws of the land. Unfortunately for most of the English people, this document meant nothing since they were serfs, so they still had no rights at all. Still, the Magna Carta was **a step in the right direction**. It gave people more rights than ever before.

In the 1700s and 1800s, philosophers started to talk about natural rights. Natural rights are not based on the laws or customs of any particular culture or government; they are universal and **absolute**. Natural rights include the right to life and liberty (freedom). Philosophers thought people had these rights **by nature**, that is, by the very fact that they are human beings. These ideas became very popular. When the American colonies decided to **separate from** Great Britain (the American Revolution: 1775-1783), it talked about these rights. Thomas Jefferson wrote that everyone was **equal** and had natural rights including the right to life, freedom and happiness. After the French Revolution (1789-1799), the people of France talked about similar rights.

During this time, many authors wrote about human rights. These writings were very popular. People like Gandhi in India and Martin Luther King Jr. in the U.S. read these writings. They helped these men to come up with their own ideas about how people should be treated. Gandhi **ended up freeing** India from English rule, and Martin Luther King began the process of advancing the civil rights of African Americans.

At first, these ideas of human rights were not too specific. People did not think about them too much. However, as technology improved and people's lives became easier and more relaxed, it became more important for everyone to be able to live well. Technology also gave people the ability to **harm** or kill many more people much more quickly and easily. Because people had both more leisure time and had seen what technology could do **in the wrong hands**, they began to think more about human rights.

Human rights became especially important after World War II, when so many people died. After entire cities had been destroyed and the horrors of the holocaust, people began to demand that every government gives all its people human rights. This is why the United Nations made so many **statements** about human rights after World War II including the Universal Declaration of Human Rights.

Today, many organizations, such as Amnesty International and Human Rights Watch, work to protect human rights. They work with governments around the world to change their actions. They also make lists of governments that do not give their people human rights. This helps force governments to change.

Additionally, people are beginning to talk about new rights. For example, the right to a clean environment is more important than ever before. People believe everyone should have the right to clean water and air. This is changing how people talk about human rights.

Human rights have changed a lot over the past four hundred years. Long ago, few people had human rights, but today international law says that all people should be given civil and political rights. They can live without government interference in their lives, and they can participate in the government of their country, mainly by voting. Most people also agree that everyone deserves economic, social and cultural rights. These include the right to education, housing, a good standard of living and healthcare services. Perhaps, someday soon, everyone will also have new rights, including the right to a clean environment.

*freeman: a person who is entitled to citizenship

*serf: a slave who is required to render services to a lord, commonly attached to the lord's land and transferred with it from one owner to another

*holocaust: an event in which many people are killed

Basic Skills Focus

■ RECALL FACTS

1. Who had human rights in ancient Rome? Write the number "1" in the passage.

2. Who did the Magna Carta help? Write the number "2" in the passage.

3. When did the idea of natural rights become popular? Write the number "3" in the passage.

4. How do Amnesty International and Human Rights Watch help people who are not being given their human rights? Write the number "4" in the passage.

5. What is a new human right some people think everyone should have? Write the number "5" in the passage.

■ IDENTIFY FACTS

1. Which of the following people did **NOT** work towards human rights and freedom?
   a. the King of England
   b. Thomas Jefferson
   c. Martin Luther King
   d. Gandhi

2. Which of the following is **NOT** true of the Magna Carta?
   a. The king did not want to agree to it.
   b. It said that no freeman could be punished without reason.
   c. It was written in 1215.
   d. It was the first document to grant universal human rights.

3. Which of the following was **NOT** affected by the new idea of human rights and freedoms?
   a. India separating from England
   b. allowing slaves to live in Rome
   c. the French Revolution
   d. America separating from England

4. Which of the following is **NOT** a reason people think about human rights more now than they did in the past?
   a. World War II was very destructive.
   b. People are much more civilized and intelligent now.
   c. People have easier and more relaxed lives.
   d. Technology gives people the ability to kill many people very quickly.

5. Which of the following is **NOT** true of the history of human rights?
   a. Some are trying to ensure people have new human rights.
   b. It ensures the government follows the constitution, and it guarantees its people human rights.
   c. Natural rights are those rights entitled to all men simply because they are people.
   d. Philosophers' ideas about natural rights did not become popular until after the French and American revolutions.

LESSON 6 The History of Human Rights 67

2 Reading Skills Focus

■ MAIN IDEA

1. What is the main idea of the reading?
   a. how philosophies can affect society
   b. where human rights came from
   c. why technology and free time can be dangerous

■ AUTHOR'S PURPOSE

1. The author wrote this article to _____.
   a. examine who decided everyone should have human rights
   b. explain how the idea of human rights emerged
   c. convince people which new human rights should be granted

■ DETAIL

1. When were human rights commonly understood as very important fundamental rights around much of the world?
   a. after World War II
   b. during the French Revolution
   c. when the Magna Carta was written

■ INFERENCE

1. What is one reason human rights took so long to become universal?
   a. For a long time, not all people were considered equal.
   b. Poor people did not want or need human rights through most of history.
   c. There were no revolutions before the 1700s and 1800s.

2. Why are there groups like Amnesty International and Human Rights Watch?
   a. Because someone has to fight for new rights like the right to a clean environment.
   b. Because governments need to see their names on lists before they will take away any rights.
   c. Because there are still places in the world where people's human rights are not recognized.

■ CONTEXT CLUE

| harm | equal | in the right direction | statements | absolute |

1. One of the principles upon which the U.S. constitution was founded is that all people are _____. Everyone is the same and should be treated with respect.

2. The Magna Carta did not give all English people human rights, but it was a step _____.

3. Natural rights are _____; that is, they are complete and without exception.

4. After World War II, the UN made many _____ about human rights. They declared a number of new international covenants.

5. Technology also has negative effects; it gave people the ability to _____ one another.

68 UNIT 3

3 Thinking Skills Focus

■ PARAPHRASING SKILLS

1. Most people say that the first human rights were written in the Magna Carta in England in 1215. The Magna Carta limited the power of the king. It was forced on King John by his most powerful subjects. It stated that no freeman, that is, anyone who was not a serf, could be punished except through the laws of the land.

   a. Human rights began with the Magna Carta. They limited the power of the king so that he could no longer punish freemen or serfs without reason.
   b. In England in 1215, the king forced his subjects to write the Magna Carta so that anyone not a serf could only be punished through law.
   c. The Magna Carta, possibly the first time human rights were written down, limited the power of the king to punish his people.

2. Natural rights are not based on the laws or customs of any particular culture or government; they are universal and absolute. Natural rights include the right to life and liberty (freedom). Philosophers thought people had these rights by nature, that is, by the very fact that they are human beings.

   a. Natural rights, including the right to life and freedom, are given to all people at all times.
   b. Laws and customs led to the idea of natural rights which came from nature.
   c. Anyone who is human deserves natural rights; life and liberty are universal and absolute.

■ CRITICAL THINKING SKILLS

1. Which of the following was most likely true of Gandhi and Martin Luther King?

   a. They believed that the slaves in Rome and the serfs in England should be freed.
   b. They used past thinking on human rights to build their own ideas and change the world.
   c. They helped get the French Revolution started with their ideas.

2. Why are groups like Amnesty International and Human Rights Watch still around if the Universal Declaration of Human Rights guarantees all people their human rights?

   a. Because the United Nations Declaration has had no effect.
   b. Because not everyone respects human rights all the time.
   c. Because there are still many democracies in the world.

■ LOGICAL REASONING SKILLS

Read the paragraph below. Then, insert the sentence in the box into the passage at one of the numbered sites by checking the appropriate number.

There, he delivered his famous "I have a dream" speech.

Martin Luther King Jr. was born in the U.S. in 1929. He was a priest who became a leader in African American's fight for civil rights. ① He preached non-violence, following the teachings of Mahatma Gandhi. ② His fight for civil rights and to end racial discrimination began in 1955, but he is most famous for organizing the March on Washington in 1963. ③ The next year he became the youngest person ever to receive the Nobel Peace Prize. ④ Unfortunately, he was killed in on April 4, 1968. The day is now a national holiday in the U.S.

4 Language Skills Focus

■ VOCABULARY DEFINITION

1. People who are ruled by a king or queen are called his or her _____.
   a. subjects　　　　　　　　　　　b. serfs

2. In the eighteenth and nineteenth centuries, philosophers began to talk about absolute natural rights. They thought all human beings had these rights _____.
   a. by voting　　　　　　　　　　b. by nature

3. A _____ is the same as a slave; he or she must work for a lord.
   a. subject　　　　　　　　　　　b. serf

4. _____, technology can be very dangerous; you do not want bad or crazy people to have access to deadly weapons.
   a. In the wrong hands　　　　　b. Specific

■ LANGUAGE FORMS

1. Very few people had human rights in the past. _____ Rome and freeman in England after the publication of the Magra Carta were the only people to have them.
   a. Citizenship of　　　　　　　　b. Citizens of
   c. Citizenship for　　　　　　　　d. Citizens for

2. _____ the surfs who lived in Rome _____ human rights.
   a. None of, did not have　　　　b. No one of, did not have
   c. None of, had　　　　　　　　 d. No one of, had

3. The issue surrounding human rights was one of the reasons the U.S. decided to try and _____ England.
   a. be separated by　　　　　　　b. separate with
   c. be separated into　　　　　　 d. separate from

4. Gandhi _____ India, while Martin Luther King helped advance the civil rights of African Americans.
   a. ended free　　　　　　　　　 b. ended up free
   c. ended freeing　　　　　　　　d. ended up freeing

5 Structure Skills Focus

■ REFERENT IDENTIFICATION

The Magna Carta limited the power of the king. It was forced on King John by his most powerful subjects. <u>It</u> stated that no freeman, that is, anyone who was not a serf, could be punished except through the laws of the land.

1. What does "it" refer to?
   a. the power
   b. the Magna Carta
   c. the laws

Today, many organizations, such as Amnesty International and Human Rights Watch, work to protect human rights. They work with governments around the world to change their actions. They also make lists of governments that do not give their people human rights. <u>This</u> helps force governments to change.

2. What does "this" refer to?
   a. protecting human rights
   b. changing their actions
   c. making lists of governments that do not give their people human rights

■ ERROR CORRECTION

1. <u>The</u> Magna Carta was <u>step in</u> the right <u>direction</u>.
   (a)   (b) (c)   (d)

2. Philosophers began <u>to talk</u> about natural <u>rights</u> <u>on</u> the 1700s <u>and</u> 1800s.
                      (a)   (b)   (c)   (d)

3. Philosophers thought people had <u>this</u> rights <u>based</u> <u>on</u> the fact <u>they</u> are human.
                                    (a)   (b)   (c)   (d)

4. For <u>most of</u> history, <u>only</u> certain people, <u>like</u> the <u>riches</u>, had human rights.
        (a)   (b)   (c)   (d)

5. <u>People's</u> <u>life</u> became easier <u>when</u> technology began <u>to improve</u>.
    (a)   (b)   (c)   (d)

6. The UN <u>made</u> so many <u>statements</u> <u>about</u> human rights after <u>the World War II</u>.
           (a)   (b)   (c)   (d)

7. Human rights <u>have changed</u> <u>a lot</u> since the <u>past</u> four <u>hundreds year</u>.
                 (a)   (b)   (c)   (d)

8. Thomas Jefferson wrote that everyone was <u>equal</u> and had natural rights
                                             (a)
   <u>include</u> the right <u>to</u> life, freedom <u>and</u> happiness.
    (b)   (c)   (d)

9. International law <u>says</u> that <u>all people</u> should <u>give</u> civil and political <u>rights</u>.
                      (a)   (b)   (c)   (d)

10. Gandhi <u>ended up</u> <u>freeing</u> India <u>from</u> <u>England</u> rule.
             (a)   (b)   (c)   (d)

LESSON 6 The History of Human Rights 71

6 Communication Skills Focus

ACCURACY SKILLS

Answer the following questions by writing full sentences. Use the clues to help you come up with the correct answer.

1. What did the Magna Carta say?
   • freeman • punished

2. What are natural rights?
   • not based on • universal and absolute

FLUENCY SKILLS

Discuss your answers with a partner. Use the clues to help you come up with the correct answer.

1. When did human rights become especially important? Why?
   • World War II • holocaust

2. When did people begin to think about human rights more?
   • technology • easier

PERSONALIZING SKILLS

Answer the following questions with your own ideas in full sentences.

1. What do you know about the history of human rights in your country?

2. How can you stop human rights abuses in North Korea?

Reinforcement Reading

Read the short passage below that expands on the reading at the beginning of the lesson. Then, cross out the unnecessary sentence by checking the box next to it.

Mahatma Gandhi was born in 1869 in Porbandar, India. ☐ He has been portrayed in literature, film and theatre. He studied law in England before returning to India in 1915. By 1921, he was a member of India's Congress. There, he led campaigns to end poverty, extend women's rights and bring different religions together. ☐ His biggest goal though, was the independence of India from England. To this end, he led non-violent marches so that he could help free India from British control. On March 12, 1930, Gandhi and 78 male activists started their marches including the 23-day-long Salt March. They took the 240-mile journey from Sabarmati to Dandi to demand an end to the British monopoly on salt. Since salt was necessary in everyone's daily diet, all the people in India were affected. ☐ Gandhi was jailed numerous times, but he always called for non-violent protests and became an inspiration for civil rights and freedom around the world. ☐ Eventually, his work paid off. India gained its independence, though not in the way he wanted. Gandhi did not want to see the country split into India and Pakistan.

Mahatma Gandhi: Champion of Human rights

7 Presentation Skills Focus

■ Give a presentation using a visual aid.

STEP 1 PLAN
Fill in the flow chart on the history of human rights as discussed in the passage.

ANCIENT ROME	• Only _____, like _____, had human rights.
ENGLAND	• _____ had human rights after _____ was published.

1700s AND 1800s	• _____ talked about _____ rights.
	• Two Revolutions:
	  The _____ Revolution: 1775-1783
	  The _____ Revolution: 1789-1799
	• Civil rights leaders including _____ in India and _____ in the U.S. began to _____.

AFTER WWII	• The _____ was so horrible that people demanded everyone receive all their _____ all the time.
PRESENT	• _____ and _____ now work to ensure everyone gets their human rights • People are beginning to talk about new _____. The _____ is an example of a new human right.

STEP 2 PREPARE
Use the "Outline" chart below to prepare your presentation about "The History of Human Rights." You may prepare an outline by making some notes in the space below.

OUTLINE		
1. Introduction	**2. Body**	**3. Conclusion**

• Attention Getter/Hook
• Statement of Topic
• Overview
  - Main Point 1
  - Main Point 2
  - Main Point 3
	• Main Point 1
	  - Examples/Evidence
	• Main Point 2
	  - Examples/Evidence
	• Main Point 3
	  - Examples/Evidence
		• Restatement of Topic
		• Main Point 1
		  - Brief Review
		• Main Point 2
		  - Brief Review
		• Main Point 3
		  - Brief Review
		• Closing Comment

STEP 3 PRACTICE
Pair up. Then, deliver your presentation to each other.

STEP 4 PERFORM
Present your completed presentation to the class. Then, complete the peer evaluation record using a scale from 1 (lowest) to 5 (highest).

PEER EVALUATION RECORD
Presenter's Name: _____

Delivery	Grade				
Posture	1	2	3	4	5
Eye Contact	1	2	3	4	5
Gestures	1	2	3	4	5
Voice Inflection	1	2	3	4	5
Content	**Grade**				
Introduction	1	2	3	4	5
Body	1	2	3	4	5
Use of Evidence	1	2	3	4	5
Conclusion	1	2	3	4	5

UNIT 3 REVIEW

INFORMATION ORGANIZATION

Fill in the timeline with all the events related to human rights mentioned in this unit. Use the approximate dates and events below to complete the diagram. Then, in each box, write a few additional details beside the name of each event about its significance as it relates to the origins of human rights.

HUMAN RIGHTS TIMELINE

500 B.C. - A.D. 500	Ancient Rome	

EVENTS AND DATES

Ancient Rome	500 B.C. - A.D. 500
Magna Carta	1215
Idea of Natural Rights	1700s-1800s
American Revolution	1775-1783
French Revolution	1789-1799
World War II	1939-1945
Universal Declaration of Human Rights	1948
Covenant on Civil and Political Rights	1976

UNIT 4

SOLAR SYSTEM

Lesson 7. The Inner Solar System

Focused Reading   Our Solar System: Inner Planets
Reinforcement Reading   Amazing Facts about NASA's Mars Rover Curiosity

Lesson 8. The Outer Solar System

Focused Reading   Our Solar System: Outer Planets
Reinforcement Reading   Interesting Facts about Comets

UNIT 4

LESSON 7.
The Inner Solar System

■ **PRE-DISCUSSION FOCUS**

 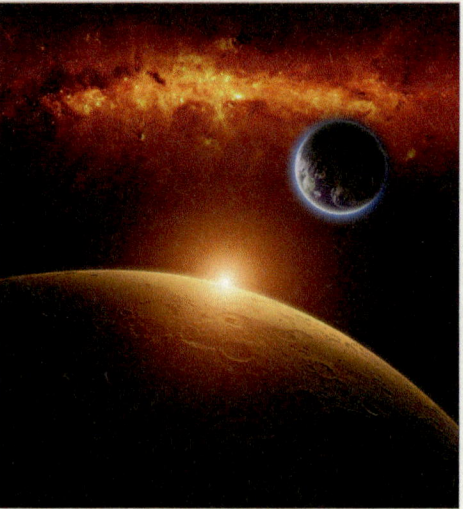

1. Do you believe in aliens? Why or why not?
   ....

2. What planets make up the inner solar system? Share your answer with a partner.

MY LIST	MY PARTNER'S LIST

■ **SCHEMA FOCUS**

Read the statements below and write **T** for true, **F** for false or **NS** for what you are not sure of.

1. Twenty percent of Americans believe in aliens. ....
2. Most of the solar system is a vacuum. ....
3. Jupiter is further away from Earth than the sun. ....
4. The sun and the moons and planets that orbit it make up our solar system. ....
5. Terrestrial planets are very dense, spin slowly and have many moons. ....

Our Solar System: Inner Planets

According to polls, 80% of Americans believe that the U.S. government knows about aliens and is hiding the information. Also, 20% of people worldwide believe that there are aliens living on Earth today. If there are aliens, though, they probably do not come from our solar system. There is some evidence of life on Mars, but anything living on Mars is probably tiny and not intelligent.

Even without green aliens with three heads, our solar system is a **fascinating** place. One of the most difficult things to understand is how large the solar system is. In fact, most of the solar system is empty space because everything is so **far apart**. This empty space is often called a **vacuum**, though it is not a true vacuum, as there are actually a few **particles** present.

To understand these distances, we can imagine the solar system on a much smaller scale. If the earth were the size of a grape, the moon would be about 30 centimeters away. The sun would be 150 meters from Earth, and Jupiter would be 600 meters away. Neptune, the farthest planet, would be almost 4.5 kilometers from Earth.

Our solar system **is made up of** the sun and everything that travels around it. This includes eight planets, at least three dwarf planets, more than one hundred planetary satellites moons, and countless **comets** and asteroids. All of the things in our solar system **circle around** the sun. They travel in nearly circular **orbits** that are determined by the sun's gravity.

A **startling** 99.8% of everything in the solar system is part of the sun. If Earth were the size of a grape, the sun would be 1.5 meters across. The sun creates an enormous magnetic field that covers the entire solar system. It is an enormous nuclear reactor. It provides all of the energy for everything in the solar system. Nothing can escape its influence.

The largest objects that travel around the sun are the eight planets. Earth is the third planet from the sun. It is one of the **terrestrial** planets. This means that it is a rocky planet. In fact, all of the planets in the inner solar system are terrestrial planets. These include, **in order** from the sun, Mercury, Venus, Earth and Mars.

NATURAL SCIENCES
Earth Science

Terrestrial planets have solid, rocky surfaces. They are very dense, and they spin slowly. None of these planets have rings, and they do not have very many moons.

Mercury and Venus are the two planets that are closer to the sun than Earth is. They do not have any moons, and they are both very hot. On both planets, temperatures are above four hundred degrees Celsius (400°C). The surprising fact is that Venus is hotter than Mercury even though it is further from the sun. This is because Venus has a very thick **atmosphere** with large amounts of carbon dioxide, and Mercury has no atmosphere at all. The thick atmosphere on Venus traps heat on the planet, and the four hundred degree temperatures cover the planet. On the other hand, at night, temperatures on Mercury go down to almost two hundred degrees below zero (-200°C).

Mars, the farthest terrestrial planet from the sun, has two moons. Mars has a thin atmosphere made up of carbon dioxide. However, most of its atmosphere probably reacted with water to form rocks millions of years ago. Mars is generally much colder than Earth. The hottest day on Mars can get up to around twenty degrees Celsius (20°C), but it can also get colder than one hundred fifty degrees below zero (-150°C) at the north and south poles.

Between Mars and Jupiter, there is a large **asteroid belt**. This is a ring of more than 750,000 asteroids that travel around the sun. One of these, Ceres, is large enough that it is known as a dwarf planet. This asteroid belt forms the border between the inner solar system and the outer solar system.

*dwarf planet: any celestial body orbiting the sun; larger than a satellite but smaller than a planet

1 Basic Skills Focus

■ RECALL FACTS

1. How many dwarf planets are there in our solar system? Write the number "1" in the passage.

2. What is the farthest terrestrial planet from the sun? Write the number "2" in the passage.

3. Why is Venus, which is further from the sun, hotter than Mars? Write the number "3" in the passage.

4. How cold does it get on Mars? Write the number "4" in the passage.

5. Where does the inner solar system end and the outer solar system begin? Write the number "5" in the passage.

■ IDENTIFY FACTS

1. Which of the following is **NOT** true of distances in our solar system?
   a. The sun is closer to Earth than Neptune.
   b. The moon is closer to Earth than any other planets.
   c. Most of the solar system is empty.
   d. Neptune is closer to Earth than Mars.

2. Which of the following is **NOT** true of the contents of our solar system?
   a. There are a lot of comets and asteroids.
   b. There are more moons than planets.
   c. There are eight planets.
   d. There are less than three dwarf planets.

3. Which of the following is **NOT** true of the sun?
   a. Nuclear reactions take place in the sun.
   b. It provides all the energy for the inner solar system, but not the outer.
   c. The sun is much bigger than Earth.
   d. The sun creates a magnetic field.

4. Which of the following is **NOT** true of the terrestrial planets?
   a. They are rocky.
   b. They spin slowly.
   c. They have rings.
   d. They are in the inner solar system.

5. Which of the following is **NOT** true of Mercury, Venus and Mars?
   a. Mars and Venus are closer to the sun than Earth.
   b. Mercury is cooler than Venus.
   c. Mars has two moons.
   d. Venus has a thick atmosphere.

2 Reading Skills Focus

■ MAIN IDEA

1. What is the main idea of the reading?
    a. an explanation of how the sun affects all the other things in the solar system
    b. an explanation of what and where things are in the inner solar system
    c. an explanation for the rocky features of the terrestrial planets

■ AUTHOR'S PURPOSE

1. The author wrote this article to ....
    a. explain how all the planets differ from one another
    b. prove that the planets move in orbit around the sun
    c. show how and why the solar system is a fascinating place

■ DETAIL

1. Which of the following is another name for a moon?
    a. comet
    b. satellite
    c. dwarf planet

■ INFERENCE

1. Why does it get so cold on Mercury at night?
    a. Because Mercury is the closest planet to the sun.
    b. Because Mercury is very hot during the day.
    c. Because Mercury does not have an atmosphere to trap heat.

2. How does a planet in the solar system revolve around the sun?
    a. It is held in its orbit by the gravitational force between the planet and the sun.
    b. It rotates slowly due to the sun's gravity.
    c. It falls into the center due to gravity.

■ CONTEXT CLUE

| fascinating | startling | atmosphere | asteroid belt | vacuum |

1. The inner planets are separated from the outer planets by the huge .... between Mars and Jupiter.

2. The gases which surround a planet make up its ....

3. When something is very interesting and attractive, we can call it ....

4. The fact that the sun makes up nearly 100% of all the "stuff" of the universe is ....

5. In a true ...., there is absolutely nothing. Space is often called this, but actually it contains a few particles.

3 Thinking Skills Focus

■ PARAPHRASING SKILLS

1. One of the most difficult things to understand is how large the solar system is. In fact, most of the solar system is empty space because everything is so far apart. This empty space is often called a vacuum, though it is not a true vacuum, as there are actually a few particles present.

   a. The solar system is enormous and very empty, though there are a few particles; therefore, it is not a true vacuum.

   b. Understanding the solar system and vacuums can be difficult as everything is so far apart.

   c. The solar system is incredibly large. Because so much of it is empty, we call it a vacuum.

2. Earth is the third planet from the sun. It is one of the terrestrial planets. Terrestrial planets have solid, rocky surface. They are very dense, and they spin slowly. None of these planets have rings, and they do not have very many moons.

   a. Earth is the only terrestrial planet with a solid, rocky surface and a single moon.

   b. Earth is a terrestrial planet, so it is dense, has a rocky surface, spins slowly and lacks rings.

   c. Terrestrial planets are dense and spin slowly, so they do not have rings or many moons.

■ CRITICAL THINKING SKILLS

1. If everything in our solar system travels in a circle around the sun, where is the sun?

   a. near the hottest planet

   b. at the center of the solar system

   c. in a line, very far from Neptune

2. Which of the following is true of planets without atmospheres?

   a. They have a lot of carbon dioxide gas.

   b. They are very cold during the day and very hot at night.

   c. They undergo huge temperature changes.

■ LOGICAL REASONING SKILLS

Read the paragraph below. Then, insert the sentence in the box into the passage at one of the numbered sites by checking the appropriate number.

It is thought to have formed from debris left over from the formation of the solar system.

The asteroid belt between Mars and Jupiter that separates the inner solar system from the outer is also known as the main belt. ① In the main belt are bodies ranging in size from a speck of dust to the four largest asteroids: Ceres, Vesta, Pallas and Hygiea. ② Ceres is big enough, 950km in diameter, to be classified as a dwarf planet like Pluto. ③ Or it could be the remains of a planet destroyed in a huge collision. Many of the asteroids in the main belt, and a few closer to Earth known as near-Earth asteroids, are rich in rare minerals and metals. ④ Some people want to catch and mine these asteroids! Nearly all the objects in our solar system, including the main belt, orbit the sun in a counter-clockwise direction, except for Halley's Comet.

4 Language Skills Focus

■ VOCABULARY DEFINITION

1. A very small part of piece of anything can be called a ....
   a. dwarf
   b. particle

2. .... are small "rocks" traveling through the solar system around the sun which have a "tail" of dust and gas.
   a. Asteroids
   b. Comets

3. The path along which something in the solar system travels around another object is its ....
   a. orbit
   b. gravity

4. .... is often used to refer only to the earth, but when referring to planets, it includes all those in the inner solar system.
   a. Terrestrial
   b. Border

■ LANGUAGE FORMS

1. All the planets in our solar system are very ....
   a. far below
   b. far from
   c. far apart
   d. further from

2. Mars' thin atmosphere .... carbon dioxide, but this planet once may have had liquid water.
   a. is mostly made up with
   b. is mostly made up of
   c. mostly made up with
   d. mostly made up of

3. The sun is at the center of the solar system, and everything else .... it.
   a. circle around
   b. circled around
   c. circling around
   d. circles around

4. Can you name the eight planets .... from the sun?
   a. in order
   b. in the order
   c. in orders
   d. by order

5 Structure Skills Focus

■ REFERENT IDENTIFICATION

The sun creates an enormous magnetic field that covers the entire solar system. It is an enormous nuclear reactor. It provides all of the energy for everything in the solar system. Nothing can escape <u>its</u> influence.

1. What does "its" refer to?

  a. the sun's

  b. an enormous magnetic field's

  c. the solar system's

Mercury and Venus are the two planets that are closer to the sun than Earth is. They do not have any moons, and they are both very hot. On both planets, temperatures are above four hundred degrees Celsius. The surprising fact is that Venus is hotter than Mercury even though <u>it</u> is further from the sun.

2. What does "it" refer to?

  a. Mercury

  b. Venus

  c. Earth

■ ERROR CORRECTION

1. <u>Did</u>(a) you know twenty <u>percent</u>(b) of people believe <u>are there</u>(c) aliens <u>on</u>(d) Earth?

2. The empty space of the solar system is not <u>a true</u>(a) vacuum, as there <u>are</u>(b) actually a few <u>particle</u>(c) <u>present</u>(d).

3. <u>Most of</u>(a) the solar system <u>is an</u>(b) empty space <u>because</u>(c) everything is <u>so</u>(d) far apart.

4. <u>If</u>(a) Earth <u>is</u>(b) the size of a grape, the moon <u>would</u>(c) be 30 centimeters <u>away</u>(d).

5. Neptune <u>is</u>(a) the <u>farther</u>(b) planet <u>from</u>(c) the <u>sun</u>(d).

6. <u>There</u>(a) <u>are</u>(b) <u>more</u>(c) one hundred moons in <u>our</u>(d) solar system.

7. <u>All of</u>(a) the planets <u>in</u>(b) the inner solar system <u>are</u>(c) terrestrial <u>planet</u>(d).

8. Terrestrial planets <u>have not</u>(a) <u>many</u>(b) moons <u>around</u>(c) <u>them</u>(d).

9. Temperatures <u>on</u>(a) Mercury <u>goes</u>(b) down to two hundred degrees <u>below</u>(c) zero <u>at night</u>(d).

10. Venus has <u>a very</u>(a) thick atmosphere with large <u>amount</u>(b) of carbon dioxide, and Mercury has <u>no</u>(c) atmosphere <u>at all</u>(d).

6 Communication Skills Focus

■ ACCURACY SKILLS

Answer the following questions by writing full sentences. Use the clues to help you come up with the correct answer.

1. What determines the orbits of all the things in our solar system?
   • sun • gravity

   ....

2. What is Mars' atmosphere like?
   • thin • made up of

   ....

■ FLUENCY SKILLS

Discuss your answers with a partner. Use the clues to help you come up with the correct answer.

1. What is a terrestrial planet?
   • rocky • dense

2. Where is the asteroid belt? What is it the boundary between?
   • Mars • Jupiter

■ PERSONALIZING SKILLS

Answer the following questions with your own ideas in full sentences.

1. Describe one interesting fact (not from the passage) you know about our solar system.

2. Have you ever seen a comet? If not, why do you think you haven't seen one?

Reinforcement Reading

Read the short passage below that expands on the reading at the beginning of the lesson. Then, cross out the unnecessary sentence by checking the box next to it.

Amazing Facts about NASA's Mars Rover Curiosity

On August 5, 2012 the Mars rover Curiosity landed on the red planet. ☐ Curiosity is a large, mobile lab, and its mission is part of NASA's effort to explore Mars. ☐ Its mission, more specifically, is to find out whether Mars ever had an environment capable of supporting life. It will do this mainly by analyzing samples of rocks and by drilling into the ground on Mars. It will be doing this in an area called the Gale crater. ☐ While Curiosity will not visit them, Mars has the largest volcano and deepest canyon in the solar system. Curiosity is not the first man-made rover on Mars, but it is the most high-tech. It carries very advanced scientific instruments. ☐ NASA estimates Curiosity will be able to explore Mars for one Martian year or 687 earth days, before it runs out of power.

7 Presentation Skills Focus

■ Give a presentation using a visual aid.

STEP 1 PLAN
Label the diagram below. Add one fact from the passage to each of the things you label.

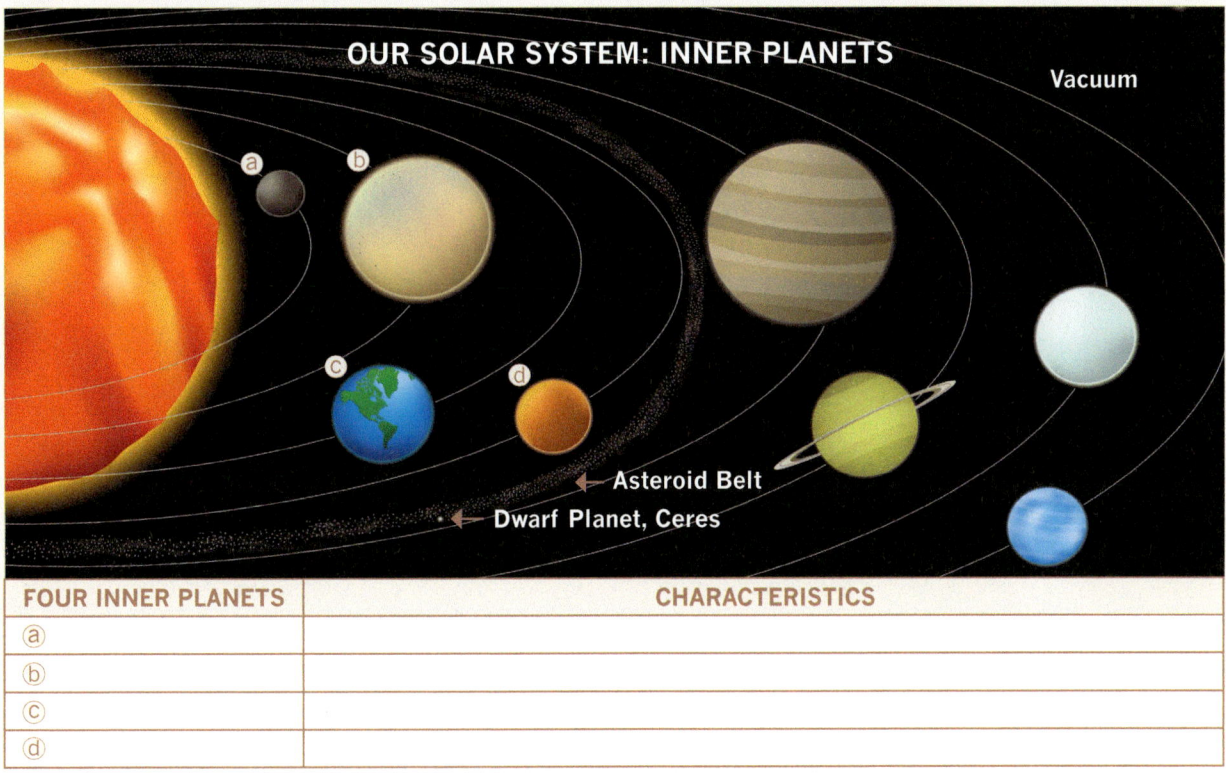

FOUR INNER PLANETS	CHARACTERISTICS
ⓐ	
ⓑ	
ⓒ	
ⓓ	

STEP 2 PREPARE
Use the "Outline" chart below to prepare your presentation about "The Inner Planets in Our Solar System." You may prepare an outline by making some notes in the space below.

OUTLINE		
1. Introduction	**2. Body**	**3. Conclusion**

• Attention Getter/Hook
• Statement of Topic
• Overview
  - Main Point 1
  - Main Point 2
  - Main Point 3
	• Main Point 1
	  - Examples/Evidence
	• Main Point 2
	  - Examples/Evidence
	• Main Point 3
	  - Examples/Evidence
		• Restatement of Topic
		• Main Point 1
		  - Brief Review
		• Main Point 2
		  - Brief Review
		• Main Point 3
		  - Brief Review
		• Closing Comment

STEP 3 PRACTICE
Pair up. Then, deliver your presentation to each other.

STEP 4 PERFORM
Present your completed presentation to the class. Then, complete the peer evaluation record using a scale from 1 (lowest) to 5 (highest).

PEER EVALUATION RECORD
Presenter's Name:

Delivery	Grade				
Posture	1	2	3	4	5
Eye Contact	1	2	3	4	5
Gestures	1	2	3	4	5
Voice Inflection	1	2	3	4	5
Content	**Grade**				
Introduction	1	2	3	4	5
Body	1	2	3	4	5
Use of Evidence	1	2	3	4	5
Conclusion	1	2	3	4	5

UNIT 4

LESSON 8.
The Outer Solar System

■ **PRE-DISCUSSION FOCUS**

1. What planets make up the outer solar system?

2. Why do you think is Pluto no longer considered a planet?

MY OPINION	MY PARTNER'S OPINION

■ **SCHEMA FOCUS**

Read the statements below and write **T** for true, **F** for false or **NS** for what you are not sure of.

1. Jupiter is the largest planet, and it has 64 moons.
2. The planets in the inner solar system are called Jovian planets.
3. The rings around Saturn are made up of rocks and dust.
4. Neptune is a blue planet because it is about the same size as Uranus.
5. Pluto used to be considered a planet.

FOCUSED READING
🎧 08

Our Solar System: Outer Planets

The outer solar system contains another four planets. These planets are called **Jovian** planets or gas giants because they have no solid surface. In other words, these planets are made up of gas instead of rock, and they are much larger than the terrestrial
5 planets. Jovian planets are like Jupiter, and they are made mainly of hydrogen and helium, although some have rock at their center. They spin more quickly, and they have very thick atmospheres. All of the Jovian planets have both **rings** and many **moons** around them.

Jupiter is the first Jovian planet. It is also the largest planet in the
10 solar system. Its rings are not very obvious, but it has sixty-four moons that circle the planet. Galileo discovered four of these moons in 1610. One of them, Ganymede, is even larger than the planet Mercury.

Jupiter has a very stormy atmosphere. Storms can last a long time on the planet. One enormous storm, like a gigantic hurricane large
15 enough to cover three Earths, can easily be seen in photographs of the planet. The storm is known as the Great Red Spot. It began before Galileo was born in 1564, and it has been raging for hundreds of years. The Great Red Spot seems to be **shrinking**, but scientists believe another major storm, now called the Little Red Spot, is forming.

20 Saturn is the second largest planet in the solar system. It has the largest rings and dozens of moons. Saturn's rings were first discovered in 1610. They are made up of dust and rocks. Some of the rocks in Saturn's rings are the size of a house. Saturn also has sixty-two moons.

When humans looked up into the night sky thousands of years
25 ago, Saturn was the farthest planet they could see. That is why the planets Mercury through Saturn are known as the **classical** planets. It is possible to see these planets without **telescopes** or **binoculars**.

Uranus was discovered in 1781 by an astronomer studying the sky with a telescope. This was the first planet to be discovered in
30 thousands of years. Uranus is unique because it **spins on its side**. All of the other planets spin at an upright angle. Uranus has twenty-seven moons and thirteen rings. Before astronomers found the rings around Uranus, they believed that only Saturn had rings. Now, astronomers know that all of the Jovian planets have rings.

NATURAL SCIENCES
Earth Science

After astronomers found Uranus, they were surprised because it did not orbit around the sun the way they thought it would. Some astronomers guessed that another planet was changing the way Uranus traveled. In 1846, the reason for Uranus' strange orbit was found – Neptune, the farthest planet from the Sun.

Neptune is about the same size as Uranus. It has several rings that seem to change frequently. Neptune has three moons. The largest moon, Triton, was found just seventeen days after astronomers found Neptune. Like Uranus, Neptune is a blue planet because its atmosphere **is full of** methane.

Until 2006, astronomers considered Pluto to be the most distant planet in the solar system. However, today astronomers call Pluto a dwarf planet. Pluto is much smaller than all of the other planets. Although Pluto has one moon, it is not large enough to control everything around it. This means that there are many other objects near Pluto that orbit the sun, not Pluto. If Pluto were a planet, it would make these objects moons, or it would **force** them into orbit.

Eris is another dwarf planet located beyond the Kuiper Belt. It is much further from the sun than Pluto. In fact, it takes Eris 557 years to travel once around the sun. That means that the last time Eris was in the same place it is now was in the 1500s. Astronomers think that Eris is about the same size as Pluto. Eris is very bright though, and astronomers think that the planet is covered in a thin **layer** of **frost**.

A third dwarf planet, Ceres, is in the main asteroid belt between Mars and Jupiter. There could be many other dwarf planets in the solar system, but dwarf planets are very difficult to find.

Comets are another important part of the solar system. They are like snowballs. They come from far beyond Neptune and move in close to the sun. As they get close to the sun, the sun melts the ice. This creates an atmosphere. Wind from the sun blows the atmosphere behind the comet. This makes it look like a fireball with a tail is flying through the sky.

The solar system is full of incredible objects traveling around the sun. Every planet and every moon is different. Comets and asteroids make our solar system an even more interesting place. Astronomers will never learn all the secrets of the solar system, but people will continue to **be fascinated by** distant and surprising places.

1 Basic Skills Focus

■ RECALL FACTS

1. When were Saturn's rings discovered? Write the number "1" in the passage.

2. Why are the planets Mercury through Saturn known as the classical planets? Write the number "2" in the passage.

3. How is Uranus unique? Write the number "3" in the passage.

4. What is Eris? Write the number "4" in the passage.

5. What are comets like? Write the number "5" in the passage.

■ IDENTIFY FACTS

1. Which of the following is **NOT** true of Jupiter?

    a. It has many red spots.

    b. It is a Jovian planet.

    c. It is hard to see its rings.

    d. There are lots of storms on it.

2. Which of the following is **NOT** true of Saturn?

    a. It has 62 moons.

    b. It is the second largest planet in our solar system.

    c. It has the largest rings.

    d. It is a classical planet because it was discovered with a telescope.

3. Which of the following is **NOT** true of Uranus?

    a. It has a strange orbit.

    b. It was discovered in 1781.

    c. It spins at an upright angle.

    d. Neptune changes how it moves around the sun.

4. Which of the following is **NOT** true of Neptune?

    a. It has an atmosphere full of methane.

    b. It is exactly the same size as Uranus.

    c. It has three moons.

    d. It has rings.

5. Which of the following is **NOT** true of Pluto?

    a. It was called a planet until 2006.

    b. The objects near Pluto orbit around it.

    c. It has one moon.

    d. It is a dwarf planet.

2 Reading Skills Focus

■ MAIN IDEA

1. What is the main idea of the reading?

    a. The classical planets were discovered before the other outer planets.

    b. The outer solar system is a fascinating place.

    c. We will never learn everything about the solar system.

■ AUTHOR'S PURPOSE

1. The author wrote this article to ....

    a. explain why Pluto is no longer considered a planet

    b. tell readers which dwarf planets can be found in the outer solar system

    c. inform readers about the outer solar system

■ DETAIL

1. Which planets are classical planets?

    a. Mercury and Saturn

    b. those in the outer solar system

    c. Mercury, Venus, Earth, Mars, Jupiter and Saturn

■ INFERENCE

1. What causes Uranus' strange orbit?

    a. the fact that Neptune's gravity was pulling on Uranus

    b. the fact that its axis is tilted much more than the other planets

    c. the fact that it spins on its side

2. What would have to happen for Pluto to be considered a planet?

    a. It would have to be less like Eris.

    b. It would have to have more than one moon and be made of hydrogen and helium.

    c. It would have to control the things around it by making them orbit around it, not the sun.

■ CONTEXT CLUE

rings	Jovian	classical	telescope	moons

1. A .... is a long cylinder that makes things appear bigger and closer than they are; it is used for looking at the stars.

2. The dust and small particles that form a disc around the Jovian planets are called ....

3. The .... planets are the ones that have been known about for the longest. They can be seen with the naked eye.

4. All the .... planets are very large, and they are made up of gas.

5. All of the planets in the outer solar system have .... in orbit around them.

3 Thinking Skills Focus

■ PARAPHRASING SKILLS

1. Astronomers call Pluto a dwarf planet. Pluto is smaller than all of the other planets. Although Pluto has one moon, it is not large enough to control everything around it. This means that there are many other objects near Pluto that orbit the sun, not Pluto. If Pluto were a planet, it would make these objects moons, or it would force them into orbit.

    a. Pluto is a small planet with one moon, and a number of other objects around it orbit the sun.
    b. Because the objects around Pluto orbit the sun, Pluto is called a dwarf planet, not a planet.
    c. Pluto is called a dwarf planet because it has one moon. Pluto and its moon orbit the sun.

2. Eris is another dwarf planet. Astronomers think that Eris is about the same size as Pluto. Eris is very bright though, and astronomers think that the planet is covered in a thin layer of frost.

    a. Eris is a small, frost-covered dwarf planet similar in size to Pluto.
    b. Astronomers do not know much about Eris because it is so far away, but they guess it is similar to Pluto.
    c. Because Eris is the same size as Pluto, it is called a dwarf planet. It is also covered in frost.

■ CRITICAL THINKING SKILLS

1. If the Jovian planets all have thick atmospheres, which of the following should be true?
    a. They should all be hot like Venus.
    b. Their temperatures during the day and the night should not be very different.
    c. They should have lots of storms on their surface.

2. Why did it take thousands of years to discover Uranus?
    a. Because it spins on its side.
    b. Because you need a telescope to see it.
    c. Because it is the first of the outer solar system planets.

■ LOGICAL REASONING SKILLS

Read the paragraph below. Then, insert the sentence in the box into the passage at one of the numbered sites by checking the appropriate number.

Enceladus is also of interest because scientists are often considering alternative places to establish new human colonies in the future outside of Earth.

　　Of Saturn's sixty-two moons, one of its most intriguing is Enceladus. Enceladus is thought by many to be the best place for humans to seek out extraterrestrial life. ① The reason for this optimism stems from the discovery of geysers located at the southern pole that shoot out streams of water ice particles into space. Some of the ice particles released become part of the rings that surround Saturn, and others fall as snow back on the surface of the moon. ② Water is the critical ingredient for life, and if water is present on this moon, there is the possibility that some other life form has evolved there. ③ In fact, NASA has recently announced that Enceladus may be the most realistic place in our solar system for humans to settle. ④

4 Language Skills Focus

■ VOCABULARY DEFINITION

1. Most people use telescopes, which have just a single lens, to look at the stars. It is also possible to see them through two lenses at once using ....
   a. angles   b. binoculars

2. Large planets are able to ...., by gravity, objects near them into orbit around them.
   a. force   b. melt

3. Because Eris is so bright, many people believe it is covered in a thin .... of frost.
   a. spot   b. layer

4. .... usually occurs on grass and plants at night when the temperature drops below freezing, but it can also occur on comets.
   a. Storm   b. Frost

■ LANGUAGE FORMS

1. One storm on Jupiter is ...., and another is just starting to form.
   a. shrank   b. shrinking
   c. shrunk   d. shrink

2. Uranus is the only planet that spins ....; it looks like the top that has fallen over but is still spinning.
   a. on its side   b. at an upright angle
   c. in its side   d. in an upright position

3. Neptune's atmosphere is .... methane, and this makes it look blue.
   a. full of   b. filled of
   c. full with   d. filled by

4. The beauty of the outer solar system's giant planets has captivated many astronomers so far, and people will continue to be .... their unrevealed secrets in the near future.
   a. fascinating of   b. fascinated to
   c. fascinating for   d. fascinated by

5 Structure Skills Focus

■ REFERENT IDENTIFICATION

In other words, these planets are made up of gas instead of rock, and they are much larger than the terrestrial planets. Jovian planets are like Jupiter, and they are made mainly of hydrogen and helium, although some have rock at <u>their</u> center.

1. What does "their" refer to?
   a. terrestrial planets'
   b. Jovian planets'
   c. Jupiter's

Wind from the sun blows the atmosphere behind the comet. This makes <u>it</u> look like a fireball with a tail is flying through the sky.

2. What does "it" refer to?
   a. the sun
   b. the atmosphere
   c. the comet

■ ERROR CORRECTION

1. Jovian planets <u>are</u> made up of gas <u>instead of</u> rock, and <u>it is</u> larger <u>than</u> terrestrial planets.
   (a)   (b)   (c)   (d)

2. Jupiter <u>is</u> <u>the</u> largest planet <u>in</u> <u>a</u> solar system.
         (a) (b)   (c)(d)

3. <u>One of</u> Jupiter's <u>moon</u>, Ganymede, <u>is</u> even larger <u>than</u> the planet Mercury.
         (a)   (b)   (c)   (d)

4. A storm <u>known</u> the Great Red Spot has been <u>raging</u> for <u>hundreds</u> of <u>years</u>.
                  (a)   (b)   (c)   (d)

5. First <u>discovered</u> in 1610, <u>Saturn</u> rings <u>are made</u> up of dust and <u>rocks</u>.
              (a)   (b)   (c)   (d)

6. It is possible <u>to see</u> the classical planets <u>without</u> the <u>help</u> telescopes or binoculars.
                         (a)   (b)   (c)
         <u>or</u> binoculars.
         (d)

7. Neptune <u>is</u> a blue planet <u>because</u> <u>it's</u> atmosphere is <u>full of</u> methane.
                   (a)   (b)   (c)   (d)

8. If Pluto <u>will be</u> a planet, the objects <u>surrounding</u> it <u>would</u> become <u>moons</u>.
                  (a)   (b)   (c)   (d)

9. Comets <u>come</u> from far <u>beyond</u> Neptune and <u>move on</u> <u>close to</u> the sun.
                  (a)   (b)   (c)   (d)

10. Astronomers <u>won't</u> never be <u>able to</u> learn <u>all</u> the <u>secrets</u> of the solar system.
                         (a)   (b)   (c)   (d)

6 Communication Skills Focus

■ ACCURACY SKILLS

Answer the following questions by writing full sentences. Use the clues to help you come up with the correct answer.

1. How do the Jovian planets differ from the terrestrial planets?
   • larger • gas

   ....

2. What major change did astronomers make in 2006?
   • Pluto • no longer

   ....

■ FLUENCY SKILLS

Discuss your answers with a partner. Use the clues to help you come up with the correct answer.

1. How does Neptune affect Uranus?
   • unusual orbit • Neptune's gravity

2. Why is Pluto called a dwarf planet?
   • not large enough • objects around it

■ PERSONALIZING SKILLS

Answer the following questions with your own ideas in full sentences.

1. Which of the outer solar system planets would be the most dangerous for humans to visit?

2. Why is it important to learn as much as we can about the planets in our solar system?

Reinforcement Reading

Read the short passage below that expands on the reading at the beginning of the lesson. Then, cross out the unnecessary sentence by checking the box next to it.

Comets are small solar system bodies or SSSBs. We can distinguish them from asteroids by their coma or 'tail'. Coma are thin, fuzzy temporary atmospheres around the comet. ☐ Tails are the thin lines sometimes visible behind comets. They are a result of solar radiation and wind pushing some of the ice and dust off the surface of the comet. ☐ Asteroids are also different from comets in that they come from near Jupiter, while comets come from the outer solar system. Comets range in size from a few hundred meters to tens of kilometers. ☐ Comets have been seen in the sky since ancient times, but only about one is visible to the naked eye every year. ☐ Halley's Comet was last seen in 1986. Traditionally, they have been thought of as bad omens.

Interesting Facts about Comets

7 Presentation Skills Focus

■ Give a presentation using a visual aid.

STEP 1 PLAN
Label the planets and dwarf planets of the outer solar system in the diagram below. Also include the number of moons for each of the four planets. In addition, add one other fact from the passage to each planet.

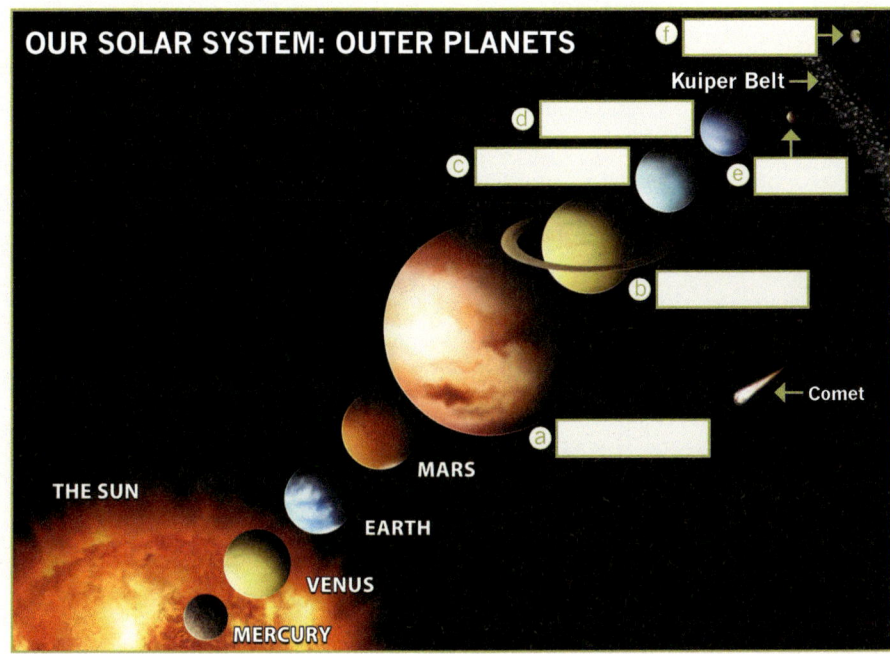
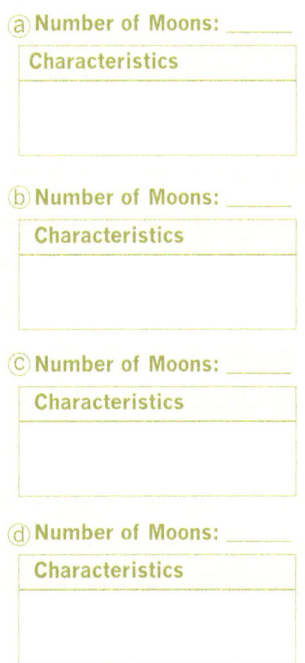

STEP 2 PREPARE
Use the "Outline" chart below to prepare your presentation about "The Outer Planets in Our Solar System." You may prepare an outline by making some notes in the space below.

OUTLINE		
1. Introduction	**2. Body**	**3. Conclusion**

• Attention Getter/Hook
• Statement of Topic
• Overview
   - Main Point 1
   - Main Point 2
   - Main Point 3
	• Main Point 1
	   - Examples/Evidence
	• Main Point 2
	   - Examples/Evidence
	• Main Point 3
	   - Examples/Evidence
		• Restatement of Topic
		• Main Point 1
		   - Brief Review
		• Main Point 2
		   - Brief Review
		• Main Point 3
		   - Brief Review
		• Closing Comment

STEP 3 PRACTICE
Pair up. Then, deliver your presentation to each other.

STEP 4 PERFORM
Present your completed presentation to the class. Then, complete the peer evaluation record using a scale from 1 (lowest) to 5 (highest).

PEER EVALUATION RECORD

Presenter's Name: ....

Delivery	Grade				
Posture	1	2	3	4	5
Eye Contact	1	2	3	4	5
Gestures	1	2	3	4	5
Voice Inflection	1	2	3	4	5
Content	**Grade**				
Introduction	1	2	3	4	5
Body	1	2	3	4	5
Use of Evidence	1	2	3	4	5
Conclusion	1	2	3	4	5

UNIT 4 REVIEW

INFORMATION ORGANIZATION

Fill in the chart below comparing the characteristics of the planets in the inner solar system to those in the outer solar system.

SOLAR SYSTEM COMPARISON CHART

CHARACTERISTICS	INNER PLANETS	OUTER PLANETS
NUMBER OF PLANETS		
NAMES OF PLANETS (in order from the sun)		
COMPOSITION (rock or mainly gas)		
RELATIVE SIZE (larger or smaller)		
SPIN SPEED		
ATMOSPHERE THICKNESS		
RINGS PRESENT OR ABSENT		
RELATIVE NUMBER OF MOONS (many or few)		

UNIT 5

TRADE IN THE PAST AND MODERN TIMES

Lesson 9. The Silk Road
Focused Reading The Legacy of the Silk Road
Reinforcement Reading Marco Polo: Silk Road Traveler and Explorer

Lesson 10. Protectionism vs. Free Trade
Focused Reading Global Exchange: Protectionism and Free Trade
Reinforcement Reading Challenges for China in the World Trade

UNIT 5

LESSON 9.
The Silk Road

■ **PRE-DISCUSSION FOCUS**

1. What do you know about the Silk Road?
   ....

2. Think about possible reasons why a particular trade route may become more popular. Write your ideas on the left side. Then, think about reasons why it may become less popular and write them on the right side. After you have read the story, refer back to your chart and see if any of your answers were correct.

REASONS FOR INCREASING POPULARITY	REASONS FOR DECREASING POPULARITY

■ **SCHEMA FOCUS**

Read the statements below and write **T** for true, **F** for false or **NS** for what you are not sure of.

1. International trade began with boats.
2. Trade routes are used to exchange both goods and ideas.
3. The Silk Road began in China and made its way to Europe.
4. The Silk Road was a safe and easy route between East and West.
5. Besides silk, various goods, technology, ideas, art, culture and religions were traded along the Silk Road.

The Legacy of the Silk Road

The **Silk Road** was a series of **trade routes** between China and Europe. There was trade between China and Europe long before there were cars, jets or even strong ships. It began almost three thousand years ago with just a few **traders** in China. Traders and goods from China
5 moved further west until they finally met up with people from Europe moving east. Among the many people to travel and trade along the Silk Road, Marco Polo may have been the most famous.

The Silk Road between China and Europe was about ten thousand kilometers long. Because it was too far for one person to travel, traders
10 only went part of the way. Then, they would sell their items to someone else. That person would take them further and sell them again. By the time a Chinese item arrived in Europe, it was very expensive. Many items did not **make it all the way** because someone in the middle decided to buy them and keep them. That is why many pieces of Chinese silk have
15 been found in tombs in the desert.

In addition to the sale of goods, religious ideas also traveled along the Silk Road. Buddhism started in India and later traveled to China along the road. Christianity also moved towards China on the Silk Road. **Missionaries** traveled to China in the 500s and 600s. They **converted** some groups in
20 the west of China to Christianity.

Travel on the Silk Road was extremely difficult. Thieves were everywhere. They stayed by the sides of the roads and tried to steal from traders. Sometimes, these thieves would kill the traders and take their items to sell. Furthermore, there was a very dangerous desert in western
25 China called the Taklamakan Desert. This desert is one of the most difficult places in the world to live. Large mounds of sand are picked up by the wind and moved across the desert. The desert is bordered on the west and south by high mountains which can only be passed on very dangerous narrow trails.

30 The Silk Road was not just one long road. There were many routes between China and Europe, but there were three main ones. All of them started in China and passed the Taklamakan Desert. From there, the northern route went to the Black Sea. The central route went to Persia, and the southern route went to India.

BUSINESS & ECONOMICS
Economics

In the beginning, there were not many towns nor was there a good system for trading along the Silk Road. Slowly, trade increased when traders started selling to people traveling across the Asian deserts. Later, the Chinese began traveling further west. The road did not yet reach Europe, but precious stones and hairy camels were traded as far as Babylon in Iraq.

Much later, around 53 B.C., the Romans found out about silk when they **conquered** the Parthians. Because not much of it got all the way to Rome, the Romans thought it was more **valuable** than gold. They were very interested in obtaining more silk for its texture, beauty and symbol of status, so they wanted to trade for it and find out how it was made. When Han Wudi became the **emperor** of China in 141, the Silk Road became more important. It was developed to make trade and travel easier.

Of course, the Silk Road carried much more than just silk. Spices, tea, ginger, porcelain, papermaking, printing, precious stones, gunpowder, bronze objects, iron, lacquer, peach and pear trees and many other items traveled west from China. On their way back to China, traders took larger breeds of horses, glass, ivory, aloe, pepper, gold, silver, grapes, cotton, wool, gems and perfumes.

The popularity of the Silk Road **rose and fell** through the rest of history. When the Han Dynasty **lost control of** China in the 200s, there was no longer a convenient way across China, so it became less important.

In the 500s, the Romans finally found out how silk was made. They sent some travelers to China to find out more. These travelers asked the experts many questions. These experts gave them both information and silk eggs. After that, the Romans were able to make their own silk in Rome, so trade **declined**. The Silk Road did not become important again until the T'ang Dynasty took control of China in 618. It was very useful for about three hundred years until the Christians and the Muslims began fighting, and the road became more dangerous.

Later, in the 1200s, the Mongols became very powerful. Under their leader, Kublai Khan, they were able to conquer all of the land between China and Europe, making it much easier for travelers to cross Asia safely.

Eventually, the Silk Road ended. There were three main reasons for this. First, the Mongol empire weakened, and travel across Asia became more difficult. Also, the Ming Dynasty (1368-1644) in China preferred not to trade with other countries. Finally, people began to build much larger and stronger ships. It became easier to trade by ship than **over land**.

■ RECALL FACTS

1. Why is the Taklamakan Desert difficult to cross? Write the number "1" in the passage.

2. What were the three main routes of the Silk Road? Write the number "2" in the passage.

3. What items were traded along the Silk Road? Write the number "3" in the passage.

4. During which three time periods mentioned in the passage did the Silk Road enjoy higher popularity? Write the number "4" in the passage.

5. Why did the Silk Road finally come to an end? Write the number "5" in the passage.

■ IDENTIFY FACTS

1. Which group converted the other?
   a. Europeans converted Chinese to Christianity.
   b. Indians converted Chinese to Buddhism.
   c. Missionaries were converted to Christianity.
   d. Chinese converted Indians to Buddhism.

2. In what year did the Romans finally find out how to make silk?
   a. around 53 B.C.
   b. in the 500s
   c. in 618
   d. in the 1200s

3. Which of the following is **NOT** true?
   a. Marco Polo traveled on the Silk Road.
   b. The Silk Road was difficult to travel.
   c. The Silk Road was free of religion.
   d. Goods along the Silk Road were frequently stolen.

4. Why were goods from China expensive in Europe?
   a. Because they had been bought and sold many times by the time they arrived.
   b. Because they had been stolen many times by the time they arrived.
   c. Because a few of the items traded were bought and kept in the Middle East.
   d. Because there were three routes between China and Europe.

5. In which route most trade between China and Europe is done these days?
   a. over land
   b. by ship
   c. by the Silk Road
   d. by plane

2 Reading Skills Focus

■ MAIN IDEA

1. What is the main idea of the reading?
    a. a discussion of the items traded along the Silk Road
    b. an explanation of why the Silk Road is no longer used
    c. a history of the Silk Road

■ AUTHOR'S PURPOSE

1. The author wrote this article to ....
    a. explain why China and Europe no longer trade with one another
    b. inform readers about trade along the Silk Road
    c. show that trade is not the best way for a country to develop

■ DETAIL

1. In which two times did the popularity of the Silk Road fall?
    a. The Mongol Empire and Christian-Islam wars
    b. The Han Dynasty and Mongol Empire
    c. The Han and Ming Dynasties

■ INFERENCE

1. Would the Silk Road have ended if the Mongol Empire did not weaken?
    a. No, having one group control Central Asia would have kept the road safe and effective.
    b. Yes, ships still would have been more efficient than the Silk Road.
    c. It is impossible to tell.

2. What would have made the most significant impact in reducing the popularity of the Silk Road?
    a. having more thieves on the sides of the roads
    b. the existence of a bigger desert surrounded by higher mountains
    c. the Europeans and Chinese being uninterested in one another's goods

■ CONTEXT CLUE

| traders | the Silk Road | trade routes | conquered | valuable |

1. The northern, central and southern routes are the main .... between China and Europe.

2. A greater number of people from China and Europe traveled through .... after Han Wudi became the emperor of China in the year 141.

3. By winning wars against many Central Asia countries, the Mongols .... the area and made the Silk Road safe to travel again.

4. Many of the items traded along the Silk Road were expensive and .... They included precious stones and hairy camels.

5. Many .... and travelers could finally travel along the Silk Road safely. It no longer had thieves by the sides of the road.

3 Thinking Skills Focus

■ PARAPHRASING SKILLS

1. There was trade between China and Europe long before there were cars, jets or even strong ships.

    a. Trade between Europe and China began a long time ago.
    b. Trade between China and Europe is mostly in cars, jets and ships.
    c. Trade between China and Europe began with cars, jets and ships.

2. Christianity also moved towards China on the Silk Road. Missionaries traveled to China in the 500s and 600s.

    a. Between 500 and 600 missionaries went to China along the Silk Road.
    b. Christian missionaries brought Christianity to China around 1,500 years ago.
    c. Missionaries used the Silk Road a long time ago to remove Christianity from China.

■ CRITICAL THINKING SKILLS

1. Why was silk so valuable in Rome before they learned how to make it?

    a. Because they had to trade horses and gold to get it.
    b. Because people always stole it.
    c. Because it was in short supply.

2. Why did the fact that dynasties in China lost control or that wars in Central Asia took place make the Silk Road less popular throughout history?

    a. During war, people lost interest in foreign goods.
    b. Without a dynasty in place or during a war, travel was much more dangerous.
    c. During these times, the price of silk dropped, so it was no longer worth the effort to trade.

■ LOGICAL REASONING SKILLS

Read the paragraph below. Then, insert the sentence in the box into the passage at one of the numbered sites by checking the appropriate number.

> The Silk Road began almost 3,000 years ago as a way for people in China to trade.

① Silk was probably the most remarkable thing traded, but it was far from the only thing. In time, the Silk Road became one of the world's oldest and the most important trade routes for the exchange of both information and goods between the East and West. ② Although a large desert, mountains and thieves made the routes dangerous, the Silk Road played a unique and central role in the processes of cross-cultural contact and exchange in the Old World. ③ The popularity of the Silk Road rose and fell over the centuries until the invention of large boats made it more economical to ship goods by sea, and the Silk Road finally ended. ④

4 Language Skills Focus

■ VOCABULARY DEFINITION

1. Buddhist _____ traveled and spread Buddhism in China.
   a. emperors
   b. missionaries

2. When the Mongol empire _____ the land across Asia, they lost power over the land.
   a. lost control of
   b. weakened

3. Han Wudi was one Chinese _____, or leader, who increased trade along the Silk Road.
   a. trader
   b. emperor

4. Many people in China were _____ Buddhism. They chose to believe in Buddhism instead of their own religion.
   a. converted to
   b. convinced to

■ LANGUAGE FORMS

1. The distance between China and Europe was too far for one person to _____.
   a. make them all the ways
   b. make it all the ways
   c. make them all the way
   d. make it all the way

2. The popularity and safety of the Silk Road _____ many times during its history.
   a. rise and fall
   b. rises and falls
   c. rose and fell
   d. risen and fallen

3. The number of people taking the Silk Road _____ as shipping emerged as an easier form of transportation.
   a. was declined
   b. were declined
   c. has been declined
   d. declined

4. These goods were not sent by ship. They were sent _____.
   a. by land
   b. over land
   c. through land
   d. on land

5 Structure Skills Focus

■ REFERENT IDENTIFICATION

The Silk Road was not just one long road. There were many routes between China and Europe, but there were three main ones. All of **them** started in China and passed the Taklamakan Desert.

1. What does "them" refer to?
   a. the Silk Road routes
   b. many routes between China and Europe
   c. three main ones

Much later, around 53 B.C., the Romans found out about silk when they conquered the Parthians. Because not much of it got all the way to Rome, the Romans thought it was more valuable than gold. They were very interested in obtaining more silk for its texture, beauty and symbol of status, so **they** wanted to trade for it and find out how it was made.

2. Who does "they" refer to?
   a. the Parthians
   b. a group of people
   c. the Romans

■ ERROR CORRECTION

1. The <u>popular</u> of <u>the</u> Silk Road <u>rose</u> and fell <u>through</u> history.
    (a)   (b)   (c)   (d)

2. The Silk Road <u>is</u> <u>about</u> 10,000 <u>kilometer</u> <u>long</u>.
                  (a)   (b)   (c)   (d)

3. <u>Buddhism</u> <u>start</u> <u>in</u> India and later traveled <u>to</u> China.
    (a)   (b)   (c)   (d)

4. The Taklamakan <u>Desert</u> is located <u>in</u> <u>northwest</u> <u>china</u>.
                   (a)   (b)   (c)   (d)

5. The Silk Road was not <u>just</u> <u>one</u> long road <u>in</u> China <u>to</u> Europe.
                          (a)   (b)   (c)   (d)

6. The Silk <u>Road</u> <u>from</u> China eventually <u>reached</u> <u>too</u> far as Europe.
              (a)   (b)   (c)   (d)

7. The Mongols <u>conquer</u> much <u>of</u> <u>Central</u> Asia <u>in</u> the 1200s.
                (a)   (b)   (c)   (d)

8. In the beginning, there <u>were</u> not many towns <u>nor</u> <u>there was</u> a good system
                            (a)   (b)   (c)
   for trading <u>along</u> the Silk Road.
                (d)

9. There are <u>at</u> least three <u>mainly</u> reasons <u>why</u> the Silk Road <u>ended</u>.
              (a)   (b)   (c)   (d)

10. <u>All the</u> different Silk Road <u>route</u> <u>passed</u> <u>the</u> Taklamakan Desert.
     (a)   (b)   (c)   (d)

6 Communication Skills Focus

■ ACCURACY SKILLS

Answer the following questions by writing full sentences. Use the clues to help you come up with the correct answer.

1. Why did many trade items from China never make it to Europe?
   • bought • kept

   ....

2. Why did the Silk Road fall into disuse in the 200s?
   • Han • lost control of

   ....

■ FLUENCY SKILLS

Discuss your answers with a partner. Use the clues to help you come up with the correct answer.

1. Why did the Silk Road lose importance in the early 900s?
   • fighting • dangerous

2. Why did the Silk Road finally end?
   • weakened • ships

■ PERSONALIZING SKILLS

Answer the following questions with your own ideas in full sentences.

1. What do you think was the most important item traded on the Silk Road? Why?

2. What do you think was the importance of East-West cultural exchange?

Reinforcement Reading

Read the short passage below that expands on the reading at the beginning of the lesson. Then, cross out the unnecessary sentence by checking the box next to it.

Marco Polo: Silk Road Traveler and Explorer

Marco Polo was born in 1254 in Venice, Italy. His father and uncle were traders. ☐ Marco became the most famous European traveler on the Silk Road. His trip to Asia lasted 24 years. ☐ In that time, he traveled almost 24,000 kilometers. He also met and worked for Kublai Khan before finally returning home. ☐ The Mongol Empire lasted from 1206 to 1368. Marco stayed with the Great Khan fully seventeen years. In all this time he never ceased to travel on special missions. As Marco brought him news from every country and conducted all the missions so successfully, the Great Khan used to entrust him with all the most interesting missions. Upon his return, Venice was at war, and he was thrown in prison. In prison, he wrote about his adventures in a book called *Il Milione di Marco Polo*, "The Travels of Marco Polo" in English. ☐ His account of the wealth of China, the might of the Mongol Empire and the exotic customs of India and Africa made his book the best seller.

7 Presentation Skills Focus

■ Give a presentation using a visual aid.

STEP 1 PLAN
First, write the name of each significant event below each year. Next, graph the rise and fall in popularity of the Silk Road by referring to the reading. Then, get ready to explain the events of the time to the audience.

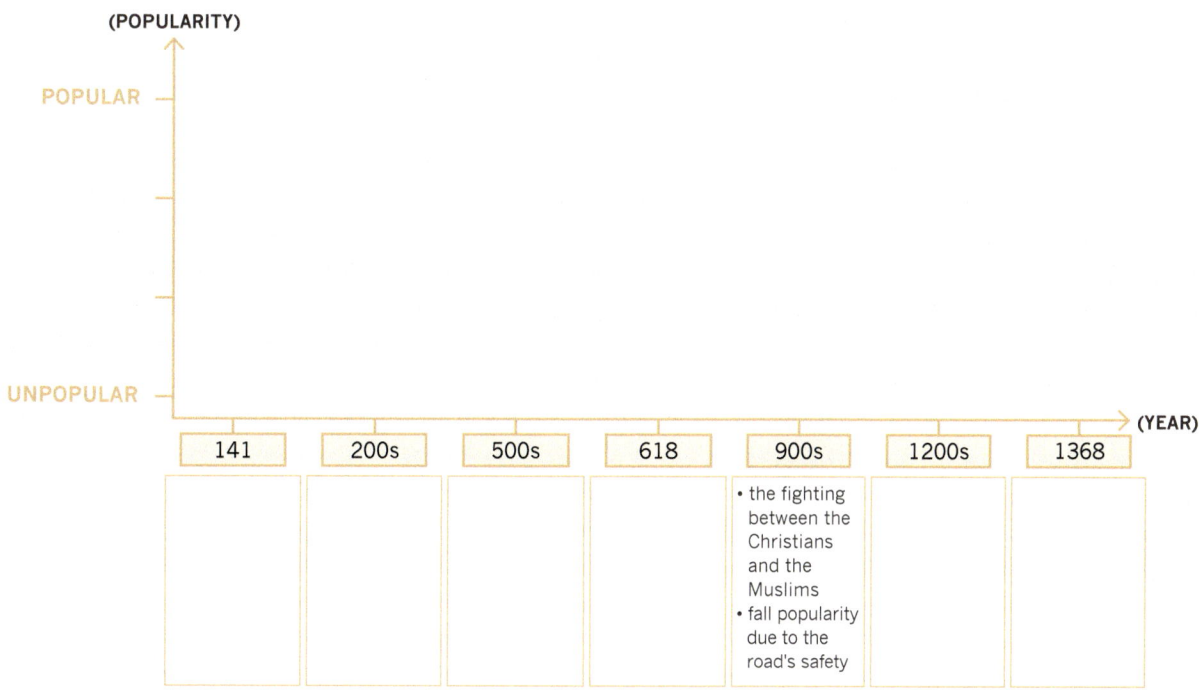

141	200s	500s	618	900s	1200s	1368
				• the fighting between the Christians and the Muslims • fall popularity due to the road's safety		

STEP 2 PREPARE
Use the "Outline" chart below to prepare your presentation about "The Rise and Fall of the Silk Road." You may prepare an outline by making some notes in the space below.

OUTLINE		
1. Introduction	**2. Body**	**3. Conclusion**

• Attention Getter/Hook
• Statement of Topic
• Overview
  · Main Point 1
  · Main Point 2
  · Main Point 3
	• Main Point 1
	  · Examples/Evidence
	• Main Point 2
	  · Examples/Evidence
	• Main Point 3
	  · Examples/Evidence
		• Restatement of Topic
		• Main Point 1
		  · Brief Review
		• Main Point 2
		  · Brief Review
		• Main Point 3
		  · Brief Review
		• Closing Comment

STEP 3 PRACTICE
Pair up. Then, deliver your presentation to each other.

STEP 4 PERFORM
Present your completed presentation to the class. Then, complete the peer evaluation record using a scale from 1 (lowest) to 5 (highest).

PEER EVALUATION RECORD
Presenter's Name: _____

Delivery	Grade				
Posture	1	2	3	4	5
Eye Contact	1	2	3	4	5
Gestures	1	2	3	4	5
Voice Inflection	1	2	3	4	5
Content	**Grade**				
Introduction	1	2	3	4	5
Body	1	2	3	4	5
Use of Evidence	1	2	3	4	5
Conclusion	1	2	3	4	5

UNIT 5

LESSON 10.
Protectionism vs. Free Trade

■ **PRE-DISCUSSION FOCUS**

1. How free and open is your country's economy?
   ....

2. Think about the advantages and disadvantages of free trade.

ADVANTAGES	DISADVANTAGES

■ **SCHEMA FOCUS**

Read the statements below and write **T** for true, **F** for false or **NS** for what you are not sure of.

1. Free trade leads to lower prices for consumers. ....
2. A quota is a type of tax which is officially allowed. ....
3. There are many ways for countries to reduce their international trade. ....
4. Protectionism means a country's economy will be stronger. ....
5. Trade was not affected by politics in the past. ....

Global Exchange: Protectionism and Free Trade

Protectionism and **free trade** are opposing economic policies nations can choose to follow in their dealings with other countries. Basically, protectionism means protecting your own industries by not allowing **competition** from other nations to enter the country. With free trade, a country opens its borders and allows in any companies and countries that want to do business in their country. The debate over which **policy** is better occurs in all countries.

A country practicing protectionism will try to **restrict** or lower trade with other countries. It does not want to buy goods from other countries, and it does not want to sell goods to other countries. These countries believe they will grow better and faster on their own.

Protectionism can be maintained in a number of ways. Countries can **impose** tariffs or quotas **on** imported goods. They can also introduce new laws and regulations. Tariffs are taxes **placed on** imported goods. The price of any item not made in the country has to include a tax, which can vary from a few percent to a doubling or tripling of the price. The money collected from the tax is collected by the government.

Quotas are another way to restrict trade. Instead of making goods more expensive, they make them less available. A quota is a "cap" or maximum number of a certain product which is allowed into the country. For example, a country may say they will only import 10,000 foreign cars. Ten thousand cars is the quota.

New laws and regulations can also make it much more difficult or even illegal to buy imported products. The government can decide that they will no longer allow certain products to be sold or products from a certain country into their market.

Tariffs, quotas and laws and regulations all **work by** making goods produced in another country more difficult to buy than the same goods produced in your country. When this happens, people are much more likely to buy **locally-made goods**. While this may make goods more expensive and be less efficient, it does mean people in the country keep their jobs, and the country maintains its industries.

If a country practices free trade, it keeps all the trade barriers low. The country tries to **eliminate** all of the policies (tariffs, quotas, laws and regulations) discussed above for protectionism. It welcomes foreign businesses and businesspeople into the country and encourages competition.

Countries with free trade **benefit from** a wider selection of lower-priced goods. Increased trade also opens new markets for their industries. On the other hand, some people may lose their jobs because the products they make can be made cheaper or better somewhere else, so everyone starts to buy from the foreign producer, and the local business closes.

In Korea, these same ideas have been discussed along with the FTA, or free trade agreement, with the U.S. The FTA will benefit Korea by opening the huge American market to Korean products. Korean businesses will be able to sell many more of their products. Korean consumers will also benefit by being able to buy products that are made more cheaply in the U.S.

Of course there are also disadvantages to the FTA. American businesses will enter the Korean market. This may mean some Korean businesses will fail if they cannot compete. Farmers in Korea are very worried about this. Rice **grown** in the U.S. is much cheaper than that grown in Korea. If American rice enters the Korean market, most people will choose to buy it, and this means that Korean farmers will lose their jobs.

Protectionism and free trade both have their advantages and disadvantages. No country is one hundred percent free or protected economically. Just how much free trade is best and how much protection is needed are questions all countries are always trying to answer. Although most economists these days argue for more free trade, the balance between the two is different for every country.

1 Basic Skills Focus

■ RECALL FACTS

1. What are three ways governments can practice protectionism?
   Write the number "1" in the passage.

2. What is the example of a quota given in the passage? Write the number "2" in the passage.

3. What is the goal of protectionism? Write the number "3" in the passage.

4. What are some of the benefits of free trade? Write the number "4" in the passage.

5. What are some of the disadvantages to Korea of a free trade agreement with the U.S.?
   Write the number "5" in the passage.

■ IDENTIFY FACTS

1. Which of the following is **NOT** true of free trade?
   a. It opens a country's borders.
   b. It protects local industries.
   c. It lowers tariffs and quotas.
   d. It means more foreign visitors.

2. How is a tariff different from a tax?
   a. They are the same.
   b. It limits the number of products imported.
   c. Tariffs only apply to imported goods.
   d. Taxes are taken by the government.

3. Which of the following is true of protectionism?
   a. Protectionism means a country does not buy goods from any other countries.
   b. Protectionism means a country buys goods from any other countries.
   c. Protectionism means a country buys and sells goods to any other countries.
   d. Protectionism means a country does not buy goods from or sell goods to any other countries.

4. If a government makes it illegal to buy, sell or own English language books, which of the following is the government using as a way to restrict trade?
   a. laws and regulations
   b. tariffs
   c. quotas
   d. taxation

5. Which of the following is **NOT** true of the Korea-U.S. free trade agreement?
   a. If cheap Korean rice enters the American market, American rice farmers will lose their jobs.
   b. Koreans will benefit from a greater selection of goods.
   c. Some Korean businesses may fail.
   d. The huge American market will be open to Korean companies.

LESSON 10 Protectionism vs. Free Trade 111

2 Reading Skills Focus

■ MAIN IDEA

1. What is the main idea of the reading?

    a. a theory on free trade

    b. an explanation of two opposing economic strategies

    c. how to save jobs and protect your country from foreign companies

■ AUTHOR'S PURPOSE

1. The author wrote this article to _____.

    a. explain protectionism and the Korea-U.S. free trade agreement

    b. show why there should no longer be any free trade agreements made

    c. explain protectionism and free trade and how they work

■ DETAIL

1. When foreign goods are of lower quality or are more expensive, what is most likely to happen?

    a. People will stop shopping and begin making things for themselves.

    b. People will buy more foreign goods to show how rich they are.

    c. People will buy more locally-made goods.

■ INFERENCE

1. In which of the following situations would a tariff be ineffective?

    a. when people only care about price

    b. when people are willing to pay a higher price for a foreign-made product

    c. when people only want to buy locally-made products

2. Which of the following is a likely outcome of free trade?

    a. Workers in wealthy countries lose their jobs to lower-paid workers in poor countries because products can be made more cheaply in poor countries.

    b. Governments make more tariffs, quotas and laws and regulations to deal with the increase in goods being traded.

    c. Economists lose their jobs because there are no more protectionist countries.

■ CONTEXT CLUE

protectionism	free trade	competition	imposed on	policy

1. Imported goods had new rules _____ them when the government restricted certain products from entering the country.

2. Allowing goods and services to move from one country to another without any limits, restrictions or taxes is called _____.

3. The economic _____ that a lot of countries debate over is protectionism and free trade.

4. By practicing _____, a country can keep its businesses safe from foreign competition and ensure that they do not fail.

5. When there are many companies making similar products, we say there is a lot of _____.

3 Thinking Skills Focus

PARAPHRASING SKILLS

1. Basically, protectionism means protecting your own industries by not allowing competition from other nations to enter the country.

    a. Protectionism is keeping foreign competition out.
    b. Protectionism means encouraging local competition.
    c. Protectionism is protecting local industries by allowing them to sell overseas.

2. Countries with free trade benefit from a wider selection of lower-priced goods. Increased trade also opens new markets for their industries.

    a. Free trade leads to new markets and more and cheaper goods.
    b. Free trade means there are more markets, so there are more goods.
    c. Free trade benefits countries by opening up good markets and giving a wider selection of markets.

CRITICAL THINKING SKILLS

1. Which of the following is **NOT** an example of protectionism?

    a. the government making safety regulations for local industries
    b. the government placing a new tariff on something imported from abroad
    c. the government making a law to limit the number of goods allowed into the country

2. Which of the following would best support the ideas about free trade?

    a. Free trade is not good for farmers because they lose their jobs.
    b. Free trade does mean some people will lose their jobs, but in the long run, it creates even more jobs.
    c. When two countries sign a free trade agreement, one country always wins, and the other country always loses.

LOGICAL REASONING SKILLS

Read the paragraph below. Then, insert the sentence in the box into the passage at one of the numbered sites by checking the appropriate number.

These countries try to reduce the barriers to trade and encourage foreign businesses to open.
---

① All countries practice some mix of protectionism and free trade. ② Countries that are more protectionist believe they need to save their workers and industries from foreign competition. ③ They do this by putting up trade barriers in the forms of tariffs, quotas and laws and regulations. Other countries believe their people will be better off with more trade and greater exchanges with other countries. ④

4 Language Skills Focus

■ VOCABULARY DEFINITION

1. The government will _____ tariffs and quotas to make trade more free.
   a. balance
   b. eliminate

2. When Korea and the U.S. signed a free trade agreement in 2007, some people thought Korea could _____ this agreement, and others thought Korean economy could be damaged.
   a. impose on
   b. benefit from

3. The tariffs _____ the imported goods will be eliminated when the free trade agreement is signed.
   a. doubled
   b. placed on

4. We have _____ on the number of apples and oranges we can import. We want to allow foreign competition, but we also need to protect local farmers.
   a. quotas
   b. tariffs

■ LANGUAGE FORMS

1. When the amount of imported food _____, farmers began producing more food.
   a. restricting
   b. was restricting
   c. restricted
   d. was restricted

2. Tariffs _____ making foreign-made products more expensive than locally-produced goods.
   a. work by
   b. work for
   c. work to
   d. work on

3. Governments practicing protectionism impose more regulations to protect _____.
   a. locally-making goods
   b. local-making goods
   c. locally-made goods
   d. local-made goods

4. Rice grown in the U.S. is cheaper than _____ in Korea.
   a. that growing
   b. growing
   c. that grown
   d. grown

5 Structure Skills Focus

■ REFERENT IDENTIFICATION

If a country practices free trade, it keeps all the trade barriers low. The country tries to eliminate all of the policies (tariffs, quotas, laws and regulations) discussed above for protectionism. **It** welcomes foreign businesses and businesspeople into the country and encourages competition.

1. What does "it" refer to?

   a. a country

   b. a country practicing protectionism

   c. a country practicing free trade

Countries with free trade benefit from a wider selection of lower-priced goods. Increased trade also opens new markets for **their** industries.

2. What does "their" refer to?

   a. countries with free trade

   b. lower-priced goods

   c. a wider selection of lower-priced goods

■ ERROR CORRECTION

1. Protectionism can work by <u>imposing</u> tariffs <u>or</u> quotas <u>on</u> <u>importing</u> goods.
                 (a)   (b)   (c) (d)

2. <u>A</u> quota is <u>maximum</u> number of <u>goods</u> <u>allowed into</u> a country.
   (a)   (b)   (c) (d)

3. The <u>new</u> tax <u>will</u> <u>be</u> collected <u>from</u> the government.
     (a) (b) (c)   (d)

4. <u>Increased</u> trade <u>open</u> new <u>markets</u> for <u>industries</u>.
   (a)   (b)   (c)   (d)

5. <u>Quota</u> are a part <u>of</u> protectionism, <u>designed</u> <u>to protect</u> local industries.
   (a)   (b)   (c)   (d)

6. Protectionism can be <u>maintained</u> <u>in</u> a number <u>of</u> <u>way</u>.
           (a) (b)   (c) (d)

7. Lowering <u>barrier</u> to trade results <u>in</u> more goods moving <u>from</u> one area <u>to</u> another.
      (a)   (b)   (c)   (d)

8. Countries with free trade <u>are benefited</u> from a wider <u>selection</u> of <u>lower-priced</u> <u>goods</u>.
          (a)   (b)   (c)   (d)

9. This <u>economist</u> is <u>arguing</u> <u>less</u> trade in order <u>to</u> reduce pollution.
      (a)   (b) (c)   (d)

10. Free trade means you <u>can</u> buy goods that <u>are</u> made more <u>cheap</u> in other <u>countries</u>.
           (a)   (b)   (c)   (d)

6 Communication Skills Focus

■ ACCURACY SKILLS

Answer the following questions by writing full sentences. Use the clues to help you come up with the correct answer.

1. If a government made it illegal to buy cars from country X, what would this be an example of?
   • example • protectionism

   ....

2. What are the advantages of protectionism?
   • protect • local

   ....

■ FLUENCY SKILLS

Discuss your answers with a partner. Use the clues to help you come up with the correct answer.

1. How is free trade different from protectionism?
   • lower • welcome

2. What is the goal of tariffs, quotas and laws and regulations?
   • buy • locally-produced

■ PERSONALIZING SKILLS

Answer the following questions with your own ideas in full sentences.

1. Which economic policy, protectionism or free trade, do you believe is better and why?

2. What do you think will be the consequences of the Korea-U.S. free trade agreement?

Reinforcement Reading

Read the short passage below that expands on the reading at the beginning of the lesson. Then, cross out the unnecessary sentence by checking the box next to it.

China is a country that has benefitted greatly from free trade. Less than 50 years ago, they were still a poor, agricultural country. ☐ Mao Zedong was the head of the communist revolution in China. Now, they are often called "the world's factory" because so many products are manufactured there. ☐ China became famous for making cheap goods and shipping them around the world. ☐ However, most consumers assumed their products were of inferior quality compared to those of their competitors. ☐ As global competition intensifies, therefore, Chinese companies have had to increase their focus on brand development and product quality. China is currently trying to change its reputation and its economy into one that makes more high-quality, high-priced goods.

Challenges for China in the World Trade

116 UNIT 5

7 Presentation Skills Focus

■ Give a presentation using a visual aid.

STEP 1 PLAN
List some advantages and disadvantages of each international trade system.

PROTECTIONISM		FREE TRADE	
ADVANTAGES	DISADVANTAGES	ADVANTAGES	DISADVANTAGES
•	•	•	•
•	•	•	•

STEP 2 PREPARE
Use the "Outline" chart below to prepare your presentation about "Free Trade vs. Protectionism." You may prepare an outline by making some notes in the space below.

OUTLINE		
1. Introduction	**2. Body**	**3. Conclusion**

• Attention Getter/Hook
• Statement of Topic
• Overview
  - Main Point 1
  - Main Point 2
  - Main Point 3
	• Main Point 1
	  - Examples/Evidence
	• Main Point 2
	  - Examples/Evidence
	• Main Point 3
	  - Examples/Evidence
		• Restatement of Topic
		• Main Point 1
		  - Brief Review
		• Main Point 2
		  - Brief Review
		• Main Point 3
		  - Brief Review
		• Closing Comment

STEP 3 PRACTICE
Pair up. Then, deliver your presentation to each other.

STEP 4 PERFORM
Present your completed presentation to the class. Then, complete the peer evaluation record using a scale from 1 (lowest) to 5 (highest).

PEER EVALUATION RECORD
Presenter's Name: _____

Delivery	Grade				
Posture	1	2	3	4	5
Eye Contact	1	2	3	4	5
Gestures	1	2	3	4	5
Voice Inflection	1	2	3	4	5
Content	**Grade**				
Introduction	1	2	3	4	5
Body	1	2	3	4	5
Use of Evidence	1	2	3	4	5
Conclusion	1	2	3	4	5

UNIT 5 REVIEW

INFORMATION ORGANIZATION

Fill in the graphic organizer with details from the passages you have read.

THE WORLD TRADE CHART: PAST AND PRESENT

HISTORY	- The Silk Road started in ....(where)........................ almost ....(when)........................ . Both .... and ideas moved along the Silk Road. Among the items traded west were .... Among those things moving east were ....
DIFFICULTY	- Describe what three things made trade along the Silk Road difficult. ① .... ② .... ③ ....
RISE AND FALL	- Describe one time when the Silk Road was popular. .... - Describe one time when the Silk Road was not popular. ....
END	- Describe three main reasons why the Silk Road ended. ① .... ② .... ③ ....

↓

MODERN TIMES	Trade is no longer carried out by people and horses. These days, huge ships sail from country to country with a lot of goods. Before it was impossible for much to be traded because it was too difficult to do. Now it is easy, but countries do not want huge quantities of foreign goods being continually brought into their countries. They need to slow trade down so that their own people and factories can still work and sell the products they make.

↓

PROTECTIONISM	Imagine you are in the government and have been tasked with figuring out how to slow trade. Explain what each of the following is and how it can reduce trade: - tariffs .... - quotas .... - laws and regulations ....

↓

FREE TRADE	Most economists these days say that free trade is the best economic policy. They say more trade means more wealth in all countries. Use the Korea-U.S. free trade agreement as an example to show both why the economist is right and why he may be wrong.

Why the economist is right:	Why the economist is wrong:
....	....
....	....
....	....

FINE ARTS & MUSIC
A History of Art and Music

UNIT 6

FROM RENAISSANCE TO BAROQUE

Lesson 11. The Renaissance Era
Focused Reading Renaissance Art and Music
Reinforcement Reading Leonardo da Vinci: The Famed Renaissance Man

Lesson 12. The Baroque Era
Focused Reading Baroque Art and Music
Reinforcement Reading Bach and Handel: The Two Giants of Baroque Music

UNIT 6

LESSON 11.
The Renaissance Era

■ **PRE-DISCUSSION FOCUS**

Leonardo da Vinci (1452-1519)

Raphael Sanzio da Urbino (1483-1520)

Michelangelo Buonarroti (1475-1564)

1. What does the word "renaissance" mean?
   ....

2. Name as many famous Renaissance artists as you can. What famous art works did they create?

NAME OF ARTIST	ART WORK

■ **SCHEMA FOCUS**

Read the statements below and write **T** for true, **F** for false or **NS** for what you are not sure of.

1. Michelangelo painted *The Mona Lisa*. ....
2. Leonardo da Vinci was one of the most influential artists of the Renaissance. ....
3. During the Renaissance, people began creating art for the church. ....
4. Renaissance art is more realistic than the art that came before it. ....
5. Renaissance "pop music" songs are known as "madrigals". ....

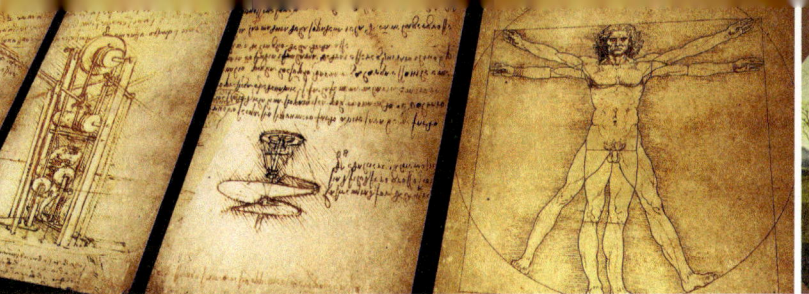

Renaissance Art and Music

The Mona Lisa (1503) is probably the most famous painting in the world. It is a portrait of a young woman looking at the viewer. People find the painting especially interesting because the woman has an enigmatic smile on her face. Many people wonder why she is smiling and what her smile means.

The Mona Lisa is a painting from the **Renaissance** (1450-1600). It was painted by Leonardo da Vinci (1452-1519). He was one of the greatest artists of the Renaissance. He also created a painting called The Last Supper (1495-1498) that shows Jesus sitting at a table with twelve of his disciples.

Another of the most outstanding artists is Michelangelo Buonarroti (1475-1564). Two of his best-known works, the Pietà (1498–1499) and David (1504), were sculpted before he turned thirty. He also painted the **ceiling** of the Sistine Chapel (1508-1512). The ceiling has many small paintings of scenes from the Christian Bible. The most famous scene is a painting of God's hand reaching out to touch the hand of Adam, the first man according to the Bible.

Before the Renaissance, most **medieval** art and music were focused on the church. Most art was inside churches and cathedrals. People wrote music so that musicians could play it in church. Most important musicians were priests and worked for the church. Both art and music were made to make the church leaders satisfied and happy. Medieval artists had **been concerned** more **with** religious symbolism than with life-like representation. They conceived of a picture as a **flat** surface on which persons or objects were shown.

The Renaissance began around the year 1450. The Catholic church was far less powerful during the Renaissance than it had been during the Middle Ages (450-1450). No longer did the church monopolize learning. Humanism strongly influenced art throughout the Renaissance. People then spoke of a "rebirth" or "renaissance" of human creativity. It was a period of curiosity, exploration, adventure and individualism.

During the Renaissance, people **were captivated by** the cultures of ancient Greece and Rome, especially the art and music of the Greeks and Romans. The Greeks and Romans had tried to make very **realistic** art because they wanted their art to look as real as possible. As people studied

FINE ARTS & MUSIC
A History of Art and Music

the Greeks and Romans, their art and music began to change. Art became much more realistic. Renaissance painters like Raphael (1483-1520) and Leonardo da Vinci were more interested in realism. They began to try to make their images look three-dimensional. This means that they painted with a new technique called "linear **perspective**," a geometrical system for creating an illusion of space and depth, so that a two-dimensional image would not look flat.

The people in the paintings also looked different. They were more active. Painters wanted to show actions. People were moving and talking to one another in the paintings while showing their emotions clearly on their faces. This made them look more comfortable than people in the older paintings. These painters were also interested in creating harmony in their paintings. They wanted their paintings to have an order that was peaceful to the eye. They tried to make the edges softer in the background.

In music, as the Greeks and Romans made theories about what sounds sounded good together and had many special ideas about how to make sounds work together **in harmony**, Renaissance composers tried to use these old theories about harmony. They created very **complicated** pieces which had many singers singing different tunes at the same time. The music was meant to create something peaceful and beautiful. Composers did not use any sounds that might sound uncomfortable. Every moment of every piece was made to sound beautiful and smooth.

Unfortunately, the music by Renaissance composers, such as Palestrina (1526-1594), was not easy to understand. One of his most famous mass was *the Pope Marcellus Mass* (1562-1563), and it was written for an a cappella choir of six voice parts: soprano, alto, two tenors and two basses. Because six singers usually sang four different tunes at the same time, it was hard to understand the words. This was even true of the pop songs of the time, called **madrigals**.

However, since there was no musical accompaniment required at first, madrigals were popular with the public because anyone could participate. They were often love songs, and it was easy to buy and sell them in the market. After a while, these songs began to become more realistic. Composers used music to show the meanings of some of the words.

Over time, artists and musicians became tired of Renaissance ideas. Artists felt that their art looked more real, but it did not show emotions well. Many people thought that Renaissance art even looked a little bit still. New artists wanted to make art that was more emotional and had more **energy**, which became the beginning of the **Baroque** style.

enigmatic: mysterious and difficult to understand

1 Basic Skills Focus

■ RECALL FACTS

1. What is the name of the famous painting that shows a woman's enigmatic smile? Write the number "1" in the passage.

2. What were Michelangelo's two famous sculptures? Write the number "2" in the passage.

3. When did the Renaissance begin in Europe? Write the number "3" in the passage.

4. Who did Renaissance artists use as inspiration for their "new" styles of art? Write the number "4" in the passage.

5. Why is Renaissance music not so popular or famous? Write the number "5" in the passage.

■ IDENTIFY FACTS

1. What did music and art in Europe focus on before the Renaissance?
    a. emotion
    b. the church
    c. harmony
    d. realism

2. Which of the following is **NOT** true of the Renaissance Era?
    a. The church was far less powerful.
    b. People were less interested in adventure and exploration.
    c. People focused on a rebirth of human creativity.
    d. Leonardo da Vinci painted *The Mona Lisa* and *The Last Supper*.

3. Which of the following was **NOT** something Renaissance artists were interested in?
    a. making their art look real
    b. having the sounds of their music work together in harmony
    c. showing emotions well
    d. making three-dimensional images

4. Which of the following is **NOT** true of Renaissance music?
    a. Composers were interested in making comfortable sounds.
    b. It was not easy to understand because singers sang different tunes simultaneously.
    c. Madrigals were the pop songs of the time.
    d. Composers invented new theories about harmony.

5. Which of the following is **NOT** a reason for the Baroque Era following the Renaissance Era?
    a. People did not want to work for the church any longer.
    b. Artists grew tired of Renaissance ideas.
    c. People wanted art with more emotion and energy.
    d. Renaissance art looked a bit still.

2 Reading Skills Focus

■ MAIN IDEA

1. What is the main idea of the reading?
    a. how the art and music of Renaissance are different from those of the Middle Ages
    b. why Renaissance music is no longer popular
    c. a history of the Renaissance period

■ AUTHOR'S PURPOSE

1. The author wrote this article to ....
    a. explain why Renaissance artists were better than the Baroque artists
    b. explain the origins and the goals of Renaissance art and music
    c. explain how harmony was involved in Renaissance music

■ DETAIL

1. Where did the inspiration for Renaissance art and music come from?
    a. the Greeks and Romans
    b. the church
    c. Da Vinci and Michelangelo

■ INFERENCE

1. What is implied in the passage about Renaissance art and music?
    a. People created more obvious emotion.
    b. People probably received music education in schools associated with churches and cathedrals.
    c. People became intoxicated with the beauty of ancient languages.

2. Why was the music of Renaissance composers not so popular?
    a. Because too many singers sang the same tunes repeatedly.
    b. Because complicated pieces made their lyrics hard to understand.
    c. Because most musical pieces were available at the market.

■ CONTEXT CLUE

| Renaissance | Baroque | perspective | madrigals | medieval |

1. Renaissance music was too complicated for many people to enjoy, but most people liked ....

2. Originated in Italy in the 17th century, ... art showed movement and emotion.

3. Renaissance painters emphasized balance and used .... to create an illusion of depth.

4. One way we can learn about music in the Middle Ages is by examining .... art.

5. .... literally means "rebirth." It usually refers to the revival of art and learning in Europe beginning in the 14th century.

3 Thinking Skills Focus

■ PARAPHRASING SKILLS

1. Art became much more realistic. Artists painted with a new technique called "linear perspective" so that a two-dimensional image would not look flat.

   a. Flat two-dimensional images are more realistic.

   b. A new technique made two-dimensional images look more flat.

   c. The style of art became three-dimensional and more realistic.

2. Unfortunately, the music by Renaissance composers, such as Palestrina (1526-1594), was not easy to understand.

   a. Renaissance music was hard to understand.

   b. Palestrina made Renaissance music, but he was hard to understand.

   c. It is easy to see why Renaissance composers were so famous.

■ CRITICAL THINKING SKILLS

1. If the Baroque Era started because "artists and musicians became tired of Renaissance ideas," why do you think the Renaissance Era began?

   a. They were bored of Greek and Roman ideas.

   b. People got tired of making art and music only for the church.

   c. They wanted to do something besides copying the styles of Da Vinci and Michelangelo.

2. Which of the following is most likely true of Greek and Roman art?

   a. It was all based on religion.

   b. It was active and three-dimensional.

   c. It was not very realistic.

■ LOGICAL REASONING SKILLS

Read the paragraph below. Then, insert the sentence in the box into the passage at one of the numbered sites by checking the appropriate number.

Michelangelo, whose full name is Michelangelo di Lodovico Buonarroti Simoni, was born in 1475 in Italy.

---

① He was a sculptor, painter, architect, poet and engineer. ② He was a Renaissance man. During his life, he was considered the greatest living artist. People called him "Il Divino" or "the divine one." He is still considered to be one of the best of all time. ③ In his lifetime, he produced a huge number of works of art, as well as writings and other projects. ④ Besides painting the ceiling of the Sistine Chapel, he created the famous statue of *David* and designed much of St. Peter's Basilica in Vatican City.

4 Language Skills Focus

■ VOCABULARY DEFINITION

1. The Sistine Chapel is a church room located in Vatican City. It is famous for its .... which has many famous paintings by Michelangelo and others.
   a. ceiling
   b. cathedral

2. Due to more movement and stronger emotion, many people see Baroque art as having more .... than Renaissance art.
   a. harmony
   b. energy

3. Basically, a .... piece of art is one that looks very life-like.
   a. religious
   b. realistic

4. Renaissance artists wanted their paintings to look more three-dimensional and less ....
   a. flat
   b. emotional

■ LANGUAGE FORMS

1. Renaissance composers were .... harmony, rather than religious symbolism.
   a. concerning with
   b. concerned with
   c. concerning about
   d. concerned about

2. Humanists in Renaissance were .... the cultures of ancient Greece and Rome.
   a. captivating for
   b. captivated for
   c. captivating by
   d. captivated by

3. If two or more sounds work together and sound comfortable, they are ....
   a. of harmony
   b. of harmonious
   c. in harmony
   d. in harmonious

4. When many singers sing at the same time, the music they create is very ....
   a. complicate
   b. complicates
   c. complicating
   d. complicated

5 Structure Skills Focus

■ REFERENT IDENTIFICATION

The Mona Lisa is a painting from the Renaissance. It was painted by Leonardo da Vinci. He was one of the greatest artists of the Renaissance. He also created a painting called *The Last Supper* that shows Jesus sitting at a table with twelve of <u>his</u> disciples.

1. Who does "his" refer to?
   a. Leonardo da Vinci's
   b. Jesus'
   c. *The Mona Lisa*'s

During the Renaissance, people were captivated by the cultures of ancient Greece and Rome, especially the art and music of the Greeks and Romans. The Greeks and Romans had tried to make very realistic art because <u>they</u> wanted their art to look as real as possible. As people studied the Greeks and Romans, their art and music began to change.

2. Who does "they" refer to?
   a. people in the Renaissance Period
   b. the Greeks and Romans
   c. ancient people

■ ERROR CORRECTION

1. <u>The Mona Lisa</u> is a <u>portrait</u> <u>of</u> a young woman <u>looked</u> at the viewer.
      ⓐ   ⓑ ⓒ   ⓓ

2. <u>Many</u> people want <u>to</u> know <u>why</u> Mona Lisa is <u>smiles</u>.
     ⓐ   ⓑ   ⓒ   ⓓ

3. <u>Over time</u>, artists <u>and</u> musicians <u>become</u> <u>tired of</u> Renaissance ideas.
       ⓐ   ⓑ   ⓒ   ⓓ

4. Madrigals <u>was</u> very popular <u>because</u> anyone <u>could</u> <u>sing</u> them.
                ⓐ   ⓑ   ⓒ ⓓ

5. <u>During</u> <u>the</u> Renaissance Period, no <u>longer</u> <u>the church did</u> monopolize learning.
      ⓐ   ⓑ   ⓒ   ⓓ

6. In music, composers <u>tried</u> to <u>using</u> the <u>old</u> theories <u>about</u> harmony.
                             ⓐ   ⓑ   ⓒ   ⓓ

7. Composers did not use <u>any</u> <u>sounds</u> <u>that</u> might sound <u>uncomfortably</u>.
                                ⓐ   ⓑ   ⓒ   ⓓ

8. The artists <u>tried</u> to make the edges <u>soft</u> everywhere, but even <u>softest</u> <u>in</u> the background.
              ⓐ   ⓑ   ⓒ ⓓ

9. The Greeks and Romans <u>had tried</u> <u>to</u> <u>make</u> <u>very</u> <u>realism</u> art.
                                   ⓐ   ⓑ   ⓒ   ⓓ

10. Every <u>moment</u> of every piece <u>was</u> made <u>sound</u> beautiful and <u>smooth</u>.
             ⓐ   ⓑ   ⓒ   ⓓ

6 Communication Skills Focus

■ ACCURACY SKILLS

Answer the following questions by writing full sentences. Use the clues to help you come up with the correct answer.

1. What was art and music focused on before the Renaissance?
   • the church

2. Who did Renaissance artists base their work on?
   • Greeks • Romans

■ FLUENCY SKILLS

Discuss your answers with a partner. Use the clues to help you come up with the correct answer.

1. Why were madrigals so popular?
   • no musical accompaniment • buy and sell

2. What did Renaissance painters want in their paintings?
   • real • harmony

■ PERSONALIZING SKILLS

Answer the following questions with your own ideas in full sentences.

1. Why do you think Renaissance artists based their work on the ancient Greeks and Romans?

2. How do you think you create harmony in a painting? How do you give it a "peaceful order"?

Reinforcement Reading

Read the short passage below that expands on the reading at the beginning of the lesson. Then, cross out the unnecessary sentence by checking the box next to it.

The Renaissance gave us the term "Renaissance Man." A Renaissance Man is someone who is an expert in many fields. ☐ Another word for Renaissance Man is polymath. This comes from the Greek "polymathes" which literally means "having learned much." These people should have a broad base of knowledge. They should study and master numerous fields. ☐ Perhaps the best example of a Renaissance Man is Leonardo da Vinci. He was a master of art, an engineer and an anatomy expert who also studied other fields. ☐ In order to become a Renaissance Man, one was expected to know several languages, understand philosophy and science, be able to appreciate art and literature, and be good in sports. ☐ Michelangelo was admired by hundreds of people at this time.

Leonardo da Vinci: The Famed Renaissance Man

7 Presentation Skills Focus

■ Give a presentation using a visual aid.

STEP 1 PLAN
Put the goals under the correct heading for the Renaissance Period.

RENAISSANCE ART	RENAISSANCE MUSIC

ⓐ real   ⓑ harmony   ⓒ active   ⓓ avoid uncomfortable sounds

ⓔ three-dimensional   ⓕ peaceful   ⓖ show emotion   ⓗ smooth

STEP 2 PREPARE
Use the "Outline" chart below to prepare your presentation about "Renaissance Art and Music." You may prepare an outline by making some notes in the space below.

OUTLINE		
1. Introduction	**2. Body**	**3. Conclusion**

• Attention Getter/Hook
• Statement of Topic
• Overview
  - Main Point 1
  - Main Point 2
  - Main Point 3
	• Main Point 1
	  - Examples/Evidence
	• Main Point 2
	  - Examples/Evidence
	• Main Point 3
	  - Examples/Evidence
		• Restatement of Topic
		• Main Point 1
		  - Brief Review
		• Main Point 2
		  - Brief Review
		• Main Point 3
		  - Brief Review
		• Closing Comment

STEP 3 PRACTICE
Pair up. Then, deliver your presentation to each other.

STEP 4 PERFORM
Present your completed presentation to the class. Then, complete the peer evaluation record using a scale from 1 (lowest) to 5 (highest).

PEER EVALUATION RECORD
Presenter's Name: ....

Delivery	Grade				
Posture	1	2	3	4	5
Eye Contact	1	2	3	4	5
Gestures	1	2	3	4	5
Voice Inflection	1	2	3	4	5
Content	**Grade**				
Introduction	1	2	3	4	5
Body	1	2	3	4	5
Use of Evidence	1	2	3	4	5
Conclusion	1	2	3	4	5

UNIT 6

LESSON 12.
The Baroque Era

■ **PRE-DISCUSSION FOCUS**

1. What do you know about Baroque art and music?
   ....

2. How can artists and musicians make their work more emotional?

ARTISTS	MUSICIANS

■ **SCHEMA FOCUS**

Read the statements below and write **T** for true, **F** for false or **NS** for what you are not sure of.

1. Baroque art had more energy and stronger emotions than Renaissance art. ....
2. Baroque art and music had a lot in common. ....
3. Baroque artists are not as famous as Renaissance artists. ....
4. Baroque music was made to be similar to the way people talk. ....
5. Baroque music included parts that were not peaceful so that the moments of harmony were even more emotional. ....

Baroque Art and Music

From some time around the year 1600, painters began to use a new style. During the Baroque Era (1600-1750), many artists created paintings with energy and strong colors. They did this to show strong emotions and make their works different from those of the Renaissance, which often **lacked** emotion. The backgrounds of their paintings were very dark with browns and blacks, but the main part of the painting had bright light. There was a lot of **contrast**. Artists became interested in forming a total illusion, like a stage setting. They used their materials to expand the dramatic potential of color, depth and contrasts of light and dark. They wanted to create totally structured worlds.

Such a style was well suited to the wishes of the **aristocracy**. The aristocracy was enormously rich and powerful during the seventeenth and eighteenth centuries. While most of the population barely managed to survive, they surrounded themselves with luxury. There were many such rulers, and they exercised absolute power over their subjects.

At the time, most people thought the style of Baroque art was very **strange**. *Baroque* is a Portuguese word meaning "imperfect or irregular shaped **pearl**," and "very unusual." People thought that Baroque art focused too much on drama. They thought it made every emotion too strong. In the Baroque Era, many great paintings were made, but none became as famous as Renaissance paintings. Baroque art was often less **celebrated** because many of its artists worked to **recreate** the art of Renaissance masters.

However, there were many famous composers from that time. The two giants of Baroque composition were Johann Sebastian Bach (1685-1750) and George Frideric Handel (1685-1759). Bach was a German Baroque musician and wrote many pieces of church music. He also wrote six very famous pieces for a small orchestra called the *Brandenberg Concertos* (1721). Handel was also a prolific British composer and liked to write opera, but his most famous work is an oratorio called *Messiah*.

Baroque art and music had a lot in common. They both tried to create a more emotional art form. Also, they both used details to make these emotions more obvious and stronger. People became very interested in Baroque music even though they did not use the word *baroque* to describe it until many years later.

Baroque music was first created in Florence, Italy. A group of musicians there wanted to have more emotional music, so they created a completely new style of music. They used just one **tune** with softer sounds in the background. They also made this tune more **similar to** the way people spoke. They tried to make sure it would be easy to understand the words.

Over time, by making music to show and explain the words, music completely changed. A new form of music, called opera, began to develop. In opera, people sang through a whole story. Sometimes they sang beautiful songs to show their talent. Other times they sang words to a special tune. This tune was very similar to the way people talked.

Even in other forms of music, Baroque composers tried to **blend** different musical ideas together. They liked harmony, but they did not expect every moment to have harmony. They tried to make some moments that were not peaceful. These moments made the peaceful moments seem much more emotional. They enjoyed making people **respond to** their work with strong emotions, and they wanted to surprise people. They used contrast as a dramatic element.

Baroque composers even used one very unusual way to surprise people with music. They wrote music that would sound special in a certain building. Many Baroque musical pieces were performed in churches. These churches were usually built in the shape of a *T*. Baroque composers had **parts of** the choir or orchestra stand in different parts of the building to make the sound even more special.

The Renaissance and Baroque Eras had very different art and music. There were many great musicians and composers during the Renaissance. There were also many great artists during the Baroque Era. However, these times featured very different ideas. These ideas changed the way people understood these artists and composers. The art and music of the Renaissance used the ideas of the ancient Greeks and Romans. It tried to be very peaceful and show emotion in well-balanced ways. Over time, however, people wanted more obvious emotion. Artists created Baroque art with strong energy and strong colors. Musicians created new music forms with more contrast and more emotion. Both of these styles used many **decorations** to make their work more emotional. In different ways, art and music both responded to the needs of the times.

1 Basic Skills Focus

■ RECALL FACTS

1. How did Baroque artists show emotion? Write the number "1" in the passage.

2. What does the word *baroque* mean? Write the number "2" in the passage.

3. What was Handel's most famous work? Write the number "3" in the passage.

4. What type of music resulted from making music to show and explain the words? Write the number "4" in the passage.

5. Where was a lot of Baroque music written to be preformed? Write the number "5" in the passage.

■ IDENTIFY FACTS

1. Which of the following is **NOT** true of Baroque music?
   a. It was meant to be emotional.
   b. It always had harmony.
   c. It used just one tune.
   d. It was made to be easy to understand.

2. Which was **NOT** mentioned as a reason why Baroque art was not as popular as Renaissance art?
   a. Because it focused too much on drama.
   b. Because many Baroque artists only worked to recreate the art of Renaissance masters.
   c. Because it was not colorful enough to show strong emotion.
   d. Because it was way too emotional.

3. How did Baroque artists and composers try to create more emotion?
   a. They used details.
   b. They made music that went out of harmony at times.
   c. They used strong colors.
   d. They made music that was more similar to the way people speak.

4. Which of the following is **NOT** true of Baroque music?
   a. It was written to be performed in concert halls.
   b. It was more emotional than Renaissance music.
   c. It blended different musical ideas together.
   d. They used just one tune with softer sounds in the background.

5. Which of the following is **NOT** a reason people thought Baroque art was "very unusual"?
   a. It focused on drama.
   b. It did not have many celebrated artists.
   c. It tried to surprise people.
   d. It was very emotional.

2 Reading Skills Focus

■ MAIN IDEA

1. What is the main idea of the reading?
    a. how Baroque art is different from Renaissance art
    b. why Baroque artists were not as talented as those in the Renaissance
    c. what characteristics Baroque art and music share

■ AUTHOR'S PURPOSE

1. The author wrote this article to _____.
    a. teach readers about the Baroque Era
    b. explain how Baroque art was different from Renaissance art
    c. show readers what Baroque art and music had in common

■ DETAIL

1. Why did Baroque composers include moments that were not peaceful?
    a. Because they only used one tune.
    b. Because they wanted to make the peaceful moments seem even more emotional.
    c. It was the result of blending different musical ideas together.

■ INFERENCE

1. What is the general feeling of the Baroque Era suggested by the passage?
    a. It was not nearly as good or productive as the Renaissance Era.
    b. It had great artists who could copy any of the masters, but the music was too emotional and lacked harmony so it never became popular.
    c. It had its strong points and created important new ideas, but it was considered strange so it was not very appreciated.

2. What happens when music is created with just one tune, has softer sounds in the background and is similar to how people talk?
    a. You get an era in which there are no famous artists.
    b. You get music which is easier to understand.
    c. You get music very similar to opera.

■ CONTEXT CLUE

| recreate | lacked | contrast | tune | blend |

1. Baroque music tried to _____ different musical ideas together.

2. Paintings with very dark and very light colors are the examples of _____.

3. Baroque artists created more emotional pieces, which _____ in Renaissance paintings.

4. The melody of a piece of music is its _____.

5. Many Baroque artists tried to _____ the masterpieces of the Renaissance.

3 Thinking Skills Focus

■ PARAPHRASING SKILLS

1. From some time around the year 1600, painters began to use a new style. During the Baroque Era, many artists created paintings with energy and strong colors.

   a. Baroque art used new paints to create energetic styles.
   b. Painters loved the new energy and strong colors of Baroque music.
   c. Baroque art featured energy and strong colors.

2. Baroque music was first created in Florence, Italy. A group of musicians there wanted to have more emotional music, so they created a completely new style of music.

   a. Baroque music was emotional and completely new.
   b. A group of emotional Italians wanted to make new music in Florence.
   c. More emotional music means that a new style was created.

■ CRITICAL THINKING SKILLS

1. Which of the following would be the best definition of "contrast" in Baroque art?

   a. art which emphasizes differences
   b. art which is imperfect or unusual
   c. art which includes harmony

2. Which of the following was **NOT** something which made Baroque music special?

   a. It blended different musical ideas together.
   b. It was similar to how people spoke, so it was easy to understand.
   c. It preferred harmony to contrast.

■ LOGICAL REASONING SKILLS

Read the paragraph below. Then, insert the sentence in the box into the passage at one of the numbered sites by checking the appropriate number.

It had just one tune, and that was easier to understand.

The Renaissance, or rebirth of art and music, began around 1400 in Europe. Renaissance art and music were no longer made only for the church. They were based on the ideas of the ancient Greeks and Romans. ① They wanted to make three-dimensional, active and emotional art. They wanted peaceful and harmonious music. By 1600 people were getting tired of the Renaissance ideas of art. ② The Baroque Era began with artists making pieces with more energy and strong emotions. ③ Although many people found the art a little strange, many great composers lived at this time. They made music that was more emotional. ④ They also made their music surprising, and it did not always have to be peaceful and in harmony.

4 Language Skills Focus

■ VOCABULARY DEFINITION

1. Baroque and Renaissance artists use lots of .... to make their work more emotional.
   a. harmony
   b. decorations

2. A .... is a smooth, white bead and also part of what the word *baroque* means.
   a. pearl
   b. opera

3. Baroque art is less ...., less well-known and praised less than that of the Renaissance.
   a. celebrated
   b. well-balanced

4. The .... saw the dramatic style of Baroque architecture and art as a means of impressing visitors and expressing triumphant power and control.
   a. subjects
   b. aristocracy

■ LANGUAGE FORMS

1. Because the Baroque style of painting was so new and different, a lot of people ....
   a. find it strange
   b. find them strangely
   c. found it strange
   d. found them strangely

2. Opera's tune is more .... the way people speak than any of the music from the Renaissance.
   a. same to
   b. same as
   c. similar to
   d. similar as

3. People need different things at different times. Art and music often .... whatever it is people feel a need for.
   a. respond with
   b. respond from
   c. respond by
   d. respond to

4. .... the choir in a Baroque concert stand and sing in different areas to create a unique sound.
   a. Part of
   b. Parts of
   c. All of
   d. All

136 UNIT 6

5 Structure Skills Focus

■ REFERENT IDENTIFICATION

From some time around the year 1600, painters began to use a new style. During the Baroque Era, many artists created paintings with energy and strong colors. They did **this** to show strong emotions and make their works different from those of the Renaissance, which often lacked emotion.

1. What does "this" refer to?
   a. creating paintings with energy and strong colors
   b. showing strong emotions
   c. lacking emotion

Most people thought the style of Baroque art was very strange. *Baroque* is a Portuguese word meaning "imperfect or irregular shaped pearl," and "very unusual." People thought that Baroque art focused too much on drama. They thought **it** made every emotion too strong.

2. What does "it" refer to?
   a. imperfect pearl
   b. Baroque art
   c. drama

■ ERROR CORRECTION

1. The Renaissance <u>and</u> Baroque <u>Era</u> <u>had</u> <u>very</u> different art and music.
         (a)   (b) (c) (d)

2. <u>People</u> <u>in</u> the Baroque Era <u>wanted</u> <u>obviouser</u> emotion.
    (a) (b)   (c) (d)

3. <u>Renaissance</u> and Baroque art and music <u>either</u> responded to the <u>needs</u>
    (a)   (b)   (c)
   of the <u>times</u>.
      (d)

4. Baroque <u>musical</u> <u>pieces</u> <u>were</u> performed <u>by</u> churches.
      (a) (b) (c)   (d)

5. Because many churches were <u>build</u> in the <u>shape of</u> a *T*, different sounds
              (a)   (b)
   <u>could</u> be made by moving the singers around <u>within</u> the building.
    (c)   (d)

6. Baroque composers did not expect every <u>moment</u> of <u>their</u> music to <u>having</u>
                  (a)   (b)   (c)
   <u>harmony</u>.
    (d)

7. The <u>aristocracy</u> was <u>enormously</u> rich and powerful during the <u>seventeen and</u>
     (a)   (b)   (c)
   <u>eighteen</u> <u>centuries</u>.
       (d)

8. Some <u>Italian</u> musicians <u>wanted</u> <u>to</u> have more <u>emotion</u> music.
      (a)   (b) (c)   (d)

9. While most people are familiar <u>with</u> Renaissance artists <u>like</u> Da Vinci, <u>little</u>
              (a)   (b)   (c)
   people can name <u>any</u> Baroque artists.
         (d)

10. Baroque <u>artists</u> <u>used</u> strong <u>colors</u> <u>to showing</u> emotion.
        (a) (b)   (c) (d)

6 Communication Skills Focus

■ ACCURACY SKILLS

Answer the following questions by writing full sentences. Use the clues to help you come up with the correct answer.

1. How did Baroque painting show contrast?
   • backgrounds • main part

   ....

2. Why is Baroque art less celebrated than Renaissance art?
   • recreate • masters

   ....

■ FLUENCY SKILLS

Discuss your answers with a partner. Use the clues to help you come up with the correct answer.

1. What did Baroque art and music have in common?
   • emotional • details

2. What unusual way did Baroque artists employ to surprise their audiences?
   • special • building

■ PERSONALIZING SKILLS

Answer the following questions with your own ideas in full sentences.

1. Do you like to sing in the shower? How does this idea relate to the passage on Baroque artists?

2. What do you think of opera? Do you agree with how it is described in the passage?

Reinforcement Reading

Read the short passage below that expands on the reading at the beginning of the lesson. Then, cross out the unnecessary sentence by checking the box next to it.

Bach and Handel: The Two Giants of Baroque Music

Johann Sebastian Bach and George Frideric Handel are two of the most famous Baroque Era composers. Bach was from Germany. ☐ He came from a musical family. While growing up, he learned to play the violin, harpsichord and clavichord. He was also an accomplished singer. Later on, he became a music teacher and composer for royalty. Among Bach's most famous works are the *Brandenburg Concertos* and the *Mass in B minor*. ☐ Handel was born in the same year (1685) as Bach. While his family was not musical, he went on to become a most famous Baroque composer. ☐ In 1750 he was seriously injured in a carriage accident in the Netherlands, soon after one of his eyes began to fail, and eight years later he died a rich and famous man. Handel is best known for oratorios. ☐ His works include *Water Music, Music for the Royal Fireworks* and *Messiah*.

7 Presentation Skills Focus

■ Give a presentation using a visual aid.

STEP 1 PLAN
First, fill in the Venn diagram comparing Baroque art and music. Then, put whatever features they have in common in the area of overlapping circles.

BAROQUE ART		BAROQUE MUSIC

STEP 2 PREPARE
Use the "Outline" chart below to prepare your presentation about "Baroque Art and Music." You may prepare an outline by making some notes in the space below.

OUTLINE		
1. Introduction	**2. Body**	**3. Conclusion**
• Attention Getter/Hook • Statement of Topic • Overview - Main Point 1 - Main Point 2 - Main Point 3	• Main Point 1 - Examples/Evidence • Main Point 2 - Examples/Evidence • Main Point 3 - Examples/Evidence	• Restatement of Topic • Main Point 1 - Brief Review • Main Point 2 - Brief Review • Main Point 3 - Brief Review • Closing Comment

STEP 3 PRACTICE
Pair up. Then, deliver your presentation to each other.

STEP 4 PERFORM
Present your completed presentation to the class. Then, complete the peer evaluation record using a scale from 1 (lowest) to 5 (highest).

PEER EVALUATION RECORD
Presenter's Name: _____

Delivery	Grade				
Posture	1	2	3	4	5
Eye Contact	1	2	3	4	5
Gestures	1	2	3	4	5
Voice Inflection	1	2	3	4	5
Content	**Grade**				
Introduction	1	2	3	4	5
Body	1	2	3	4	5
Use of Evidence	1	2	3	4	5
Conclusion	1	2	3	4	5

UNIT 6 *REVIEW*

INFORMATION ORGANIZATION

Based on what you have learned from the entire unit, fill in the following chart comparing the Renaissance and Baroque Eras.

A COMPARISON OF STYLES: RENAISSANCE AND BAROQUE

	THE RENAISSANCE ERA		THE BAROQUE ERA	
	ART	MUSIC	ART	MUSIC
STYLE				
INSPIRATION				
FEATURES				
FAMOUS ARTISTS				
OTHER				